# Praise for *Run Your Business Like A Fortune 100*

## Media Authorities

*"Lober's book will help you figure out what's important and what's not for growing your business and for keeping it competitive. It will help you navigate through the fog of 'information overload' to set a course for business success."*

—Rich Sabreen
Rich Sabreen Enterprises, Former Executive Vice President, Global Media at Reuters

*"Two of the most important factors in running a successful business are having a clear vision and having stakeholders who buy into that vision. Lober clearly explains how with numerous helpful cases and insights derived from Fortune 100 companies and small businesses alike."*

—Robert Levin
Editor-in-Chief & Publisher, New York Enterprise Report

*"In the era of new media and multi-distribution approaches Rosalie Lober's book provides insights and practical approaches required in the ever-changing economy. These must needed principles are a terrific resource for sustaining the profitability of your business."*

—Matthew A. Hege
Executive Vice President, The Broadway Channel

*"Woven throughout Dr. Lober's new book are numerous 'a-ha's' with respect to customer focus for entrepreneurs to ask and listen for: Can your target customer also be one of your business partners? Are your functions serving your customers or pursuing extraneous activities?"*

—Heather Myers
Senior Vice President, Strategic Planning and Business Development, Scholastic

## Finance/Legal Authorities

*"Lober's Run Your Business Like a Fortune 100 is very relevant to corporate America, small and medium-sized companies and the industry worldwide. The examples cited are easily recognized by any CEO who has been responsible for P&L and for performance improvement."*

—Wilfried Jackson
Executive Vice President, Chief Operations/Technology Officer, First Southern Bank
Former CEO National Credit Cards and Retail Bank, Citibank Nevada, NA

*"Lober is on the mark regarding the enormous investments successful companies make in developing sound processes with best practices you can use right now in 'simple to adapt' steps for increasing your profitability and focusing rigorously on the reality of your markets."*

—Bob Finkel
CFO, Metro USA,
Former Vice President Finance, CBS Television Stations

*"Lober excels in presenting vital operational insights, especially the pivotal role that integration and testing/revising plans play in a company's success. She challenges readers to link every aspect of their business to triumph in this highly competitive global marketplace."*

—G. Patrick McGunagle
COO, Pan-American Life Insurance Group
Former Managing Director, Citigroup

*"Intrapreneurs and entrepreneurs strive to exploit every opportunity to grow and use the latest technology and cut costs at the same time. These goals are usually in conflict, but Lober gives practical advice and examples for how they can all be achieved."*

—Gerard Callaghan
Managing Director, Bank of America
Former Managing Director, Citigroup

*"In these turbulent times, it's not enough to be 'good enough.' Run Your Business Like a Fortune 100 provides entrepreneurs with the very tools they need to transform their companies. The result will be a business transformation focusing on high priorities and high ROI."*

—Nina Kaufman
Ask The Business Lawyer, speaker, entrepreneur

*"Lober provides a roadmap for positioning your product to the right customers based on sound principles and a pragmatic approach to business building that helped the biggest and most successful companies become global leaders."*

—Rafi Mohammed
Author of *The Art of Pricing*
CEO, Pricing for Profit

## Venture Capital/Private Equity Authorities

*"Not since Tom Peters' in Search of Excellence has there been an analysis that aspiring entrepreneurs could put to use immediately to transform their own businesses ... a handbook to execute best practices and take companies to the next level in revenue growth & profitability."*

—Karen Rands
President, Launch Funding Network Inc., www.Launchfn.com

*"Lober reduces large corporate practices to their essence, providing entrepreneurs with an indispensable strategy to adopt the "best practices" of large corporations while preserving the unique "energy" and benefits of small to medium sized businesses."*

—David Anthony
Managing Partner, 21Ventures LLC.

*"I've experienced Dr. Lober's ability to size up a situation realistically and build strong teams. Run Your Business Like A Fortune 100 is for anyone who wants practical, proven principles and tools for growing PROFITS and running their business effectively."*

—Ian Fallmann
CEO, Kensington Enterprises Ltd.
Former Asia-Pacific MD of Bloomberg LLP

## Technology Authorities

*"Every executive needs to take Rosalie Lober's warning to stop investing in expired ideas and misguided assumptions. She asks the right questions and crafts a set of principles and framework to assess your strategy continuously. This book should be required reading."*

—Edmundo Llopis
Managing Partner Sentaire Partners
Former Executive Vice President, Citigroup

*"Lober's Run Your Business Like A Fortune 100 captures today's challenges for integrating technology, business development and operations with a plethora of realistic authentic examples of companies that struggled with these complex issues."*

—Maryellen Erica Evans
Managing Director, eNetPloy
Former COO, Optigenex Inc.

*"Lober's new book, Run Your Business Like A Fortune 100, got my attention as a creative approach to blend the best corporate practices with the simplicity and ingenuity of small companies to articulate an intuitive multifunctional discipline."*

—Guillermo Kopp
Executive Director, Fellow Tower Group
Former Regional Director, US at Citigroup

## Supply Chain and Operations Authorities

*"Dr. Lober knows how to simplify and adapt elaborate, time-consuming best practices with ease and success. With illustrations of successful companies she will persuade you that your company can move to the next level of profitability a lot faster than you ever thought possible."*

—Tony Donofrio
President, US Mgmt Services
Former Chief Supply Chain Officer, Linens N Things

*"Finally, there is a business book with enough substance to make an impact, enough examples to make it clear, and enough detail and direction to help business leaders apply these guidelines. It is clear that Dr. Lober has been in the trenches. If you want to make a difference in your business, this book is a 'must-have'. Bravo!"*

—John P. Gaulin
President, Success Force, Inc.
Former Vice President, Citigroup

## Consumer Products and Services Authorities

*It was exciting to read Dr. Rosalie Lober's book, as she demystifies the 'secrets' of successful Fortune 100 Companies for all to understand. If you want to take your business to that next level, if you are willing to open your mind, then this is a must-read."*

—Edward F. Nesta
President Luxury Experience Company, www.L-E-Company.com;
Former Vice President, GE

*"Every entrepreneur must learn Lober's "Business Change Reality Model" if they want to truly position their company for growth. Illustrations from dozens of companies can save years of trial and error fumbling and move you up the ladder of business prosperity."*

—Jonathan Soares
Founder and CEO, Q Products Inc.

## Universities and Non-profits

*"Fortune 100 firms pay millions each year to management consultants for what Dr. Lober gives you for the price of this remarkable book. Dr. Lober's book has the answers. It is a must-read for seasoned and aspiring Entrepreneurs!"*

—J. Preston Jones D.B.A.
Executive Associate Dean
H. Wayne Huizenga School of Business and Entrepreneurship

*"Rosalie Lober knows what profits a company: PROFITS! Not only the bottom-line kind, but especially her seven key PROFITS© principles. Both small and large business leaders can profit from her insights, presented in her friendly, enthusiastic manner using many stories drawn from extensive experience."*

—Tom Pyle
Executive Director, Strathmore University Foundation
Former Chairman, TerraCycle, Inc.

## Human Capital Authorities

*"Rosalie Lober shares organizational learning best practices that any business can leverage to speed up growth, change and innovation. Lober presents numerous cases in disclosing how the most successful companies become learning organizations and stay that way."*

—Louis Carter
President and CEO Best Practice Institute

*"This book distills management practices into core ingredients that maximize business value. Dr. Lober brings to life the critical people issues that 'make or break' business success. Essential reading for entrepreneurs and to capture the attention of corporate executives scrambling to leverage the next best tool."*

—Thomas Diamante, PhD
Senior Vice President, Human Capital Consulting

*"Lober gives entrepreneurs unique insight for effectively engaging their employees to focus on profitable growth, offering intimate views of conversations that entrepreneurial CEOs have about development challenges. Lober understands how bureaucracies can inhibit competitive opportunities, torpedo innovation and hurt efficiencies and break through these barriers."*

—Nancy A. May
President & CEO, The BoardBench Companies

# RUN YOUR BUSINESS LIKE A FORTUNE 100

## 7 PRINCIPLES FOR BOOSTING PROFITS

ROSALIE LOBER, PhD

WILEY

**John Wiley & Sons, Inc.**

Published by John Wiley & Sons, Inc., Hoboken, New Jersey.

Published simultaneously in Canada.

For general information on our other products and services or for technical support,
please contact our Customer Care Department within the United States at (800)
762-2974, outside the United States at (317) 572-3993 or fax (317) 572-4002.

Wiley also publishes its books in a variety of electronic formats. Some content that
appears in print may not be available in electronic books. For more information about
Wiley products, visit our web site at www.wiley.com.

***Library of Congress Cataloging-in-Publication Data:***

Lober, Rosalie.
 Run your business like a Fortune 100 : 7 principles for boosting profits/by
Rosalie Lober.
  p. cm.
 Includes bibliographical references.
 ISBN 978-0-470-39699-5 (cloth)
 1. Success in business.  2. Management.  3. Profit. I. Title.
 HF5386.L759 2009
 658.4'01–dc22

                                                        2008052150

Printed in the United States of America

10 9 8 7 6 5 4 3 2 1

*To Julia Miriam,*
*my inspiration*

# Contents

Foreword                                                    xi
Preface                                                     xv
Acknowledgments                                            xix

## Part I: PROFITS for Sustainable Growth                    1

**Chapter 1:** Achieving a Profitable Business                3

**Chapter 2:** PROFITS                                       18

**Chapter 3:** Position Only for Growth                      34

**Chapter 4:** Reality                                       55

**Chapter 5:** Obtain Vital Information                       78

**Chapter 6:** Flexibility                                   96

**Chapter 7:** Integration                                  117

**Chapter 8:** Test and Revise                              137

**Chapter 9:** Steering the Company                         152

# CONTENTS

**Part II:** **Run Your Business Like a Fortune 100—The Tools** **173**

**Chapter 10:** Business Reality Change Model     177

**Chapter 11:** People Processes     195

**Chapter 12:** Consultative Dialogue     221

**Chapter 13:** What to Do Right Now!     233

*Bibliography*     *244*
*Index*     *249*

# Foreword

No one is more passionate about helping successful entrepreneurs become great ones than my friend, Rosalie Lober, for whom I have the privilege to introduce this book. She has thought deeply about the challenges you face every day and she addresses them with originality and confidence that will move you to implement one powerful idea after another.

In good years and bad, some companies can be counted on to produce sustainable, profitable growth. They know their customers and their competitors almost as well as they know themselves. They face facts and prepare for every eventuality. They know where they are headed and communicate that direction clearly to customers, markets, staff, and investors. They adapt flexibly to change and measure what's important. They question relentlessly, and never shy away from reassessing strategy. They integrate processes, people, and departments so that all stakeholders stay aligned in pursuit of clear goals.

This book is for the successful entrepreneur whose growing company is profitable and who is ready to lead the organization to the kind of peak profitability enjoyed until now, only by the world's elite corporations. First, you must internalize the principles and use the tools you will learn about in these pages.

*Run Your Business Like a Fortune 100* borrows the best practices of great companies and puts them within easy reach of businesses like yours—profitable small—and mid-sized companies hungry for expert guidance to get to the next level of success. In *Run Your Business Like a Fortune 100,* you will discover that your company's profit-making potential is both greater and closer than you thought possible.

Great entrepreneurs spend their time skating where the ice is thinnest. Quickly sizing up risks and rewards, they hew to the barely frozen edge, leaving tiny cracks behind them that can open and swallow those who dare to follow without the same fierce discipline and intensity of purpose. Admiration for this fearlessness and determination attracts early supporters to the new business, including bellwether customers, key employees, and investors.

Then the day arrives when it becomes clear that everything that got us to this point is simply not going to take us the rest of the way. Too much chaos surrounds decision-making. Inertia overcomes initiatives. People lose sight of the goal line and fall into self-defeating patterns. Customers who seemed impervious to competitive assaults begin paying attention to sales pitches from imitators. Every meeting brings rants about the economy, the market, and a hundred other external factors that block progress. Suddenly "success" doesn't look quite as bright as you'd pictured it when you were rapidly climbing toward the light of profitability.

Some version of this scenario is inevitable in the entrepreneurial lifecycle, so if this resembles the state of your enterprise today, you are in luck. First, if you've progressed to this point, you have marketable products or services, competent employees, paying customers, and a profitable business.

Most important, you now have Rosalie Lober to guide you to the next level. The principles and tools she presents have never before been available to entrepreneurs for the small cost of a book. In fact, companies that have successfully navigated these perilous waters have invested millions of dollars and years of effort to develop them.

Lober has studied and managed, developed and implemented—and here, recorded for you—the best practices of great global companies and their successful application to the specific needs of growing companies. She has adapted these mighty processes, principles, and tools to help your company become the great engine of profitability you have always envisioned—without the expense, time, and bureaucracy associated with large organizations.

Make the time to learn from the cases, absorb the principles, and use the tools. It is likely to be the second wisest investment you will ever make.

Bennett Zucker
Principal, MediaTech Business
New York, NY

# Preface

For most of us, starting a business takes Herculean courage, intense energy, and focus. As I started writing this book, what came to mind was the Force, described in *Star Wars* as "energy ... harnessed by those with unique abilities." Yes, this is the business entrepreneur.

In my early corporate positions, tasked with designing and implementing organizational change, I lived in the world of entrepreneurs, the only executives with the inclination and authority to allow me to tamper with their organizations. Entrepreneurs thrive on exciting ideas and projects, bringing together people from diverse functions and backgrounds to bring those ideas and projects to fruition. They are also the fearless ones who streamline cumbersome processes that often get in the way of an organization's success. With corporate entrepreneurs (known as intrapreneurs), I had the good fortune to design and implement company-wide change strategies, corporate universities, cross-functional projects, performance systems, value propositions, and a myriad of other creative and successful initiatives.

This was second nature to me. My experiences in business and psychology led me to embrace a systems perspective of the

All cases in this book are based on actual people, companies, and events. Some names and details have been changed at the request of the parties and to illustrate certain teaching points more clearly.

world. Renowned psychologist Kurt Lewin viewed the individual as both the influencer and the influenced within his or her environment. The individual and the environment continually interact, creating change. In the corporate world, everywhere I looked I found abundant and varied opportunities to drive and manage change.

When Combustion Engineering, Inc. made the shift from a product focus to a market focus, it caused organizational upheaval. I saw an opening to create cross-functional teams and dialogues between top and middle management, and strengthening relationships across the company. At Citibank, I observed how corporate objectives would slip through the cracks when no single department was directly accountable for achieving them. We addressed this by implementing cross-functional task forces across divisions and developing company-wide performance systems for creating better alignment, integration, and measures across divisions.

A few years later, I experimented with applying these cumbersome processes to smaller businesses. To my amazement, doing so helped these businesses flourish and sent their profits soaring. It seemed like cheating, since all I did was simplify institutionalized best practice principles. In big companies, it was "hurry up and wait" as the higher-ups eventually decided to kill or bless initiatives. This didn't happen in small and medium-sized companies. Entrepreneurs who already achieved success in those environments were eager to follow my advice and eliminate big-company obstacles.

An irony surfaces as you apply Fortune 100 best principles and processes. You may actually exceed the accomplishments of the larger companies that designed them for their use!

Entrepreneurs know what they want, and they tend to decide quickly. Two common characteristics of successful entrepreneurs are their desire to learn and their fearlessness in taking calculated risks. Most of the time they bought into my ideas. The only resistance, which applied across all industries, seemed to be the absolute conviction to remain "uncorporate," meaning not bureaucratic, slow, and constrained by people in suits who think they know better. As an entrepreneur myself, I thoroughly understand this way of thinking.

Today you have unlimited opportunities if you are a learner—one who is innovative, quick, interpersonally adept, and a risk taker. You may enter new global markets, forming innovative supply chains all over the world for operations, distribution, and sourcing. Partnerships and alliances with suppliers and customers take whatever form you choose. Yes, with imagination and courage, you can be like Ray Kinsella in *Field of Dreams*. In this movie, you may recall, Iowa farmer Ray, who hears a voice in his cornfield tell him, "If you build it, they will come." At first, he does not understand. But when he builds a baseball field on his farm, he sees the ghosts of Chicago Black Sox players who intentionally lost the 1919 World Series and were never allowed to play again. Ray begins his journey of self-discovery, exploring his dreams, revising his priorities, and achieving his heartfelt goal.

You too can keep playing even if you lose a game or two. This book is for entrepreneurially-minded people who take risks, who win and sometimes lose, and then dust themselves off and continue playing.

While there are no silver bullets and your business is different from everyone else's, there are principles and tools developed by those who came before you that can guide you in taking smarter calculated risks. We can be like Ray Kinsella. We can hear our inner voice and build our field of dreams.

*Run Your Business Like a Fortune 100* is dedicated to you, the entrepreneur—for the respect I have for your courage, your tenacity, and your creativity.

I welcome the opportunity to contribute to your success by: (1) illuminating a path to peak profitability in a current turbulent and competitive business environment; (2) coaching you to replicate award-winning best practices of Fortune 100 companies to achieve integration, profits, and sustainable growth; and (3) guiding you through the PROFITS principles and tools for advancing your company to the next level of business prosperity.

Although each of the seven principles and tools stands on its own, they occur within an economic and political context. Within the fabric of the book are strands of today's current business complexities, including vanishing boundaries, cultural transformation, process reengineering, "flat world" thinking, collaborative communities, and customer intimacy. I believe that including all these strands where relevant, results in a richer story.

Definitions of terms used throughout *Run Your Business Like a Fortune 100* are based on personal experience. Though you may wish to add to or modify them, you will be able to understand the underlying perspective of the book using my definitions.

*Run Your Business Like a Fortune 100* provides the principles, tools, and guidance your company needs to advance right now. Add your deep personal commitment to making your company stronger, superefficient, and far more profitable than your best-case forecasts, and you're on your way to the top of your industry and, just maybe, a business magazine's high achievers club! And above all else, I truly hope this book harnesses your entrepreneurial energy as described in *Star Wars* and propels your business on its next exciting voyage.

# Acknowledgments

As I convey to you, the influences and contributions of colleagues, old friends, and new friends it is a humbling reminder to me that we are not alone. This book embraces the people and ideas of the past and of those who surround me now—and it did indeed take a village for me to conceive and deliver.

With overflowing gratitude, respect and admiration, I first and foremost thank my dear friend and colleague, Bennett Zucker, who first inspired me when I was twelve years old. His continuous caring, unwaivering dedication, and vigilant attention to the context and details of this book knew no bounds. When I got tired, he kept going.

John Gaulin, my colleague, friend, and alter ego for the past eighteen years, influenced the balance between the 'how to' and the illustrative examples of the text, with his enthusiasm and excitement in critiquing and shaping it to the standards we practice in our daily lives.

Rafi Mohammed guided me through the process of birthing a book—from writing a proposal to dealing with agents and editors and to promoting and marketing. He listened, he advised, he sometimes yelled, and always was there for me. Thank you, Heather Myers, for introducing us and for your support.

With the good fortune of meeting Steve Szaraz, through Rafi, I found a gentle soul. His firm yet kind nature, allowed me to trust him as the first to read each chapter and to make sure I stayed on track.

In addition, I would like to thank the people who endorsed this book. I worked with most of them over the years and you will find the majority of them represented in the examples throughout. I thank them for entrusting me with their businesses and their concerns, along with the numerous other senior executives and business owners with whom I have the privilege of working. Without all of you, there would be no book.

I thank Rafe Sagalyn, for his experience and wisdom, Carol Hoenig, for her facility with language, Scott Allen, for his attention to detail and friendship, Rikki and Stu Bagatell, Melissa and Matt Hege, Aaron and Helen Wurm, Dianne Niklaus for their loving support and encouragement—reviewing book covers, critiquing book titles, for reading the proposal, and so much more. Ilsa Portalatin, thank you, for your extra special friendship. Dr. Leslie Rescorla and Dr. Carol Roberts, I thank you for teaching me how to write.

Thank you to the team at Wiley for leading the publishing process from start to finish—and for guiding me in the complexity of finalizing this result.

A special thanks to my daughters, Melissa and Rikki, who shine their inner beauty, generosity, and love—making everything in my life worthwhile.

To all these wonderful people and more, I offer my deepest appreciation.

# PART I

# PROFITS for Sustainable Growth

# CHAPTER 1

# Achieving a Profitable Business

*Life is either a daring adventure or nothing.*

—Helen Keller

On a Japan Airlines flight to Tokyo, I sat next to Thomas Hewitt, CEO of Tucker Airparts. As the plane reached cruising altitude, Thomas stretched contentedly and began telling me about the purpose of his trip. He was on his way to Tokyo to meet with the owner of a holding company for a group of air carriers and related services. These subsidiaries were potential buyers of Tucker's products: reconditioned and rebuilt aircraft, avionics, and aircraft instruments.

Thomas sipped his drink, becoming thoughtful as he related how his company's fortunes had turned. Tucker's sales were falling faster than the industry average in the current difficult market. Thomas attributed the downturn to competition from companies overseas, compounded by the decline in value of the dollar.

"This potential customer in Tokyo might be just the answer to Tucker Airparts' financial problems," Thomas continued. He confided that his company had barely broken even in each of the prior three years. In the preceding 10 years, profits had grown reliably every year to an all-time record high five years ago. "Fast-forward to last month," he admitted wearily, "when the bank declined our request to renew our loan and I started looking for new markets."

Thomas had tried to persuade his skeptical business partners that global expansion, especially an aggressive move in Asia, would offset declines at home while paving the way for future growth. Thomas hoped to convince his partners by returning from this trip with an important new customer's first large purchase order.

We spent the next couple of hours talking about challenges he was likely to face in a new market. How would Tucker Airparts localize its solutions for customers in this region? What about distribution channels? How would Tucker decide what to build instead of buy, or keep rather than outsource?

Somewhere over the Pacific Ocean, we realized we would probably arrive at our destination before we could even think of all the questions and possible answers, so we decided to continue the conversation in Tokyo. When we met a few days later at Bar Guapos, Thomas seemed troubled and asked if I had business experience in his industry. Though I did not have a client in the aircraft industry, I had recently retained a new client in the shipping industry who was also losing market share and considering expansion overseas.

"At this point," I said, "she doesn't have resources in Asia, either. She is weighing whether to hire new people in an unfamiliar culture and she's unsure if this expansion will generate sufficient income from the investment required for hiring and training."

Thomas nodded and replied, "My partners have that same concern. We can develop the technical capacity, but it's not available now. They see the obstacles, while I view this as a big opportunity, especially if I can close the deal this week."

He continued, "Of course we'll need to hire someone in Tokyo to handle people issues—someone who knows local laws and the Japanese culture. It's important to have a local presence for Tucker Airparts—*critical*, really, in my view. What downside do you see in the investment if this new customer wants to work with us?" he asked me.

I considered the reality of Thomas' situation as he described it thus far, his global ambitions and especially the difference of opinion with his partners. "I'm just not sure," I replied. "I need a lot more information, and, more important, so do *you*!" Thomas agreed and I asked, "Have you noticed any relevant trends in the Japanese market, especially among your competitors based in Asia, that suggest an opportunity for Tucker to succeed here in an acceptable time frame? Might this potential customer give both of you an advantage by being your partner *as well as* your customer?" I asked. "Perhaps this could save you from having to build the entire business in this new market from the ground up."

He thought about this and replied, "I guess I viewed this primarily as a lucrative sales opportunity. Their companies have large budgets for the products and services my company provides. They also want to have close business connections with a U.S. company."

Before returning to the United States, Thomas had a series of meetings scheduled with the holding company's CEO and the general managers of the key subsidiaries. He wondered whether the discussions should turn toward developing a partnership and creation of a strong global solution encompassing air transportation and services, aircraft, parts, and instruments. "You know," he said, his enthusiasm returning, "the client might be open to a partnership that fits their own global market strategies."

We talked further about the high costs of customizing for the Asian market and the distraction it would cost him personally. He soon realized that by proposing a partnership, Tucker Airparts could negotiate from strength and be more valuable to the prospect. Previously, Thomas had not considered the costs of expansion, believing that good sales automatically result in profits. He now recognized that he could attain profitability faster by reducing or eliminating costs entirely and sharing the risk with a well-positioned partner.

## WHAT DOES THOMAS, CEO OF TUCKER AIRPARTS, HAVE TO DO WITH YOU?

Why am I telling you about Thomas? There are people like Thomas in businesses everywhere. Perhaps you are dealing with great ambiguity and change in your marketplace. As an entrepreneur, you may find that almost every decision has major financial and operational consequences.

Sometimes, like Thomas, you might be uncertain of the steps to take to improve your business. Tucker Airparts experienced 10 profitable years, but barely broke even the last three years. Thomas is personable, intelligent, and committed to his business. He seems to do everything right. He thought he had found an answer, but a few timely questions helped him grasp that he was about to run his engine right off the track.

While you may identify with Thomas's predicament, you have the opportunity to avoid making serious mistakes. That's because you can learn from successful companies that have already invested years and millions of dollars struggling through situations that confound resource-constrained entrepreneurs. These companies devised processes for taking the right path into the future and avoiding common pitfalls.

*Run Your Business Like a Fortune 100* provides seven principles (PROFITS™) and some tools for evaluating your business and making tough decisions. They have been tested by companies that stand among the world's largest and most respected. By using this approach, you ask yourself essential questions and take actions that result in attaining loyal customers. If Thomas had used these principles and tools prior to his visit to Tokyo, he would have had a clearer idea of whether his potential client was the right solution for Tucker Airparts' future.

## YOU ARE AN ENTREPRENEUR

Owning a business is difficult. Like climbing a mountain, you prepare, you advance, and sometimes you fall back before you can begin climbing again.

Your business demands your blood, sweat, tears, and finances. When business is good, it's very good. You love the natural high it gives you. Your brain keeps clicking and the world is a great place. You also obsess about achieving your goals, keeping your commitments, and listening to the constant conversations in your head about new ideas and all the responsibility you bear. Like Thomas, you may be searching for new solutions when the tide turns and your profits come to a standstill.

Perhaps you now have to deal with a competitor's new product on the market that is stealing your market share point by point. Maybe a valued employee leaves after you've invested $10,000 in her training and confided in her about your most exciting ideas for next year. Your most reliable supplier discontinues a chemical you need for your product line, and customer demand is in the triple-digit range. Business life, even as we strive with dignity and class to succeed, is usually messy and inconvenient.

Did you ever think that a big company like one of the Fortune 100 would have everything it needs to deal with every problem? Fortune 100 companies are big and have other divisions to absorb the loss of a product or even a market. They have more people and can switch gears quickly. They have the money for software to streamline processes easily. Many more Fortune 100 companies than you might think, trip over their own bureaucratic complexity than benefit from it. With many layers of management vying for support and having to approve changes, large corporate entities may have trouble delivering results, adhering to time frames, and trimming costs. And they may be slow to meet sudden competitive challenges.

Similar to reaching the summit of a mountain, attaining peak profitability is exciting. Yet it is difficult to see the other side of the mountain when you are climbing it. Like a successful mountaineer, you have a sense where the terrain may be most treacherous and you arrive at these places with as much information and as many tools as practical to manage whatever you find on your descent. This book reveals what other successful entrepreneurs grasp as they get to the other side, find another peak, or zigzag to the next mountain. The quest for profitability seems never ending; no one model is perfect and every company is distinct.

Of course, you are the best judge of what will work for you and what won't, since no one knows your company as well as you do. Throughout the book, you will find questions you can ask to challenge your thinking and customize for your business.

- How can you grow more profitable in the current turbulent and competitive business environment?
- How can you replicate award-winning best practices of Fortune 100 companies to achieve integration, profit, and sustainable growth?

## ENTREPRENEURIAL OBJECTIONS TO CORPORATE SOLUTIONS

People often say they prefer the collegial, friendly climate of smaller companies. Great ideas can percolate and become reality quickly in these environments. Many small business entrepreneurs left large companies to start their own. Jim Kravitts, previously a senior vice president of a large consumer goods company, is now CEO of a company that designs shipping containers. He states, "You just couldn't get anything done at my former company. There were too many layers, too many approvals. . . . The company was just too big, and my boss got annoyed when I asked his boss a question. My company is different. Anyone can speak to anyone else, and that's how I like it. I don't want to become bigger."

Of course, some owners and CEOs of these small and medium-sized businesses may erroneously believe their companies are too small to adopt the strategic, operational, and people processes of larger corporations. John Smarts, a former CFO, whom I spoke with at an industrial construction company, summed up this concern when he told me, "The expense, people resources, and time do not justify the corporate processes."

My experience tells me otherwise. In my initial job interview at Bloomberg L.P., the first question asked of me was how to design and adapt the "best practice" talent management systems of large, successful corporations without changing Bloomberg's small company culture. During my tenure, I learned that a growing and profitable company could value what works at larger firms without changing its open, fast-moving culture. At Bloomberg, where most people do not have titles, where there are no private offices, and where people are equally accessible at all levels, the system works.

With a goal of less than six-week cycles from design to implementation, results included improvements in many processes throughout Bloomberg L.P., as well as a new global sales process and new training programs within every division. There was no fanfare, and there were no big announcements about new initiatives. We just did the work. What I learned during this challenging and exciting time inspired me to write *Run Your Business Like a Fortune 100*.

While "big and profitable" is often associated with bureaucratic, slow, and political, it does not have to be that way. By reducing large corporate practices to their essence, many small companies can now integrate change faster, operate with little bureaucracy, and become more profitable than their more sizable competitors.

## WHAT WILL THESE CHANGES COST?

Sky High is a distributor of party supplies to party goods stores. The company's sales volume increased by 5 percent between 2007 and 2009, while profits skyrocketed from $2.6 million to $5 million. The owners of Sky High attributed the whopping $2.4

million increase to adopting and integrating large corporate best practices into its existing processes.

In 2007, Mark and Judy, co-founders of Sky High, wanted to improve the efficiency and effectiveness of their company. Having owned their business for a few years, they were comfortable with the business basics that generally tax the mental and physical energy of newly minted entrepreneurs.

They contemplated possible options for business enhancements. For example, they could reduce the prices of their party favors, they could purchase their own manufacturing equipment for key products such as balloons, they could design items for new markets, or they could continue business as usual.

In 2008, Sky High decided to adapt a few large corporate practices to find the most profitable enhancements for their company. First, Sky High employees learned more about their customers' needs. In the process, they discovered that Sky High's retail consumers tended to buy either basic or custom items. Next, Mark and Judy segmented their customers and reconfigured many of Sky High's practices to align to these purchase patterns. Along with a new pricing strategy, Sky High restructured certain processes such as logistics, sales, and vendor relationship practices. As they learned more about large corporate processes, Mark and Judy initiated support mechanisms that included conducting frequent review meetings to keep Sky High focused, monitoring progress toward goals, and establishing basic performance measures for their 70 employees. As employees gained a better understanding of the party goods business, their commitment to the company strengthened. Employee accountability increased markedly, with employees taking greater responsibility for adhering to goals and time lines.

It is important to note there is nothing extraordinary about Sky High. Mark and Judy simply wanted to improve their business. They revisited their assumptions about their customers. Had they made a change such as merely reducing a price point, this probably would have caused confusion for Sky High employees and their customers. By adapting large corporate business practices with no financial investment, Sky High was able to find untapped wealth. For Sky High, this resulted in doubling profits.

## WHY IS *RUN YOUR BUSINESS LIKE A FORTUNE 100* IMPORTANT TODAY?

Formerly profitable small and medium-sized companies are losing revenue and market share today due to the easy entry of global competitors into their industries. Countless products and services are now commodities, particularly in the computer, financial, and customer services arenas.

Scores of members of Daniel Pink's "freelancer generation" in his book *Free Agent Nation* began businesses in the late 1990s and at the start of the new millennium. His book chronicles a variety of people, many previously employed in traditional work settings, who looked for work that was more profitable and offered alternative work arrangements. Now they, too, are looking for ways to enhance their businesses and deal with global competition.

According to Jim Collins, author of *Good to Great*, "good is the enemy of great." We must continuously enhance our businesses and offer customers value-added products and services that are better, faster, and cheaper than those of our competitors. Good is just not good enough. And, because we are profitable, we may not be as observant as we can be as the global marketplace shrinks beyond our peripheral vision. Though we may be aware that change is happening, we do not always know how quickly this affects our business.

Lou Gerstner stated when he became CEO of IBM in 1993 and the company was losing billions of dollars, "Transformation of an enterprise begins with a sense of urgency. No institution will go through fundamental change unless it believes it is in deep trouble and needs to do something different to survive."

An example of a fundamental change for businesses resulted when the dot-com bubble burst. Global connectivity became a commodity. To use Malcolm Gladwell's term, the *tipping point*

**11**

for worldwide connectivity arrived and we found ourselves with a superabundance of global fiber-optic cable networks. Now all you need is a computer with the capability to connect to the Internet, and you are ready to explore information to your heart's content.

Opportunities abound for those of us who want to expand our businesses into the emerging markets—or within the United States. There are opportunities for those of us with mental and physical challenges that public workplaces may view as liabilities. There are even opportunities for those of us who start businesses with extremely limited resources. Businesses can outsource just about anything, including accounting and payroll services, supply chains, day-to-day operations and a variety of marketing, human resources, and communication expertise. In this way, big companies can act small and *small companies can act big*.

There is also a downside to having so many choices. As Thomas Friedman states in *The World Is Flat*, "we have to sort out what to keep, what to discard, what to adapt, what to adopt, where to redouble our efforts and where to intensify our focus." The implication is that unless we do this well, we will fall behind.

With more options, we also have to make decisions faster. With so many of us striving and thriving in today's business environment, *it is difficult to catch up once you fall behind*. When the mantra of the day is "you snooze, you lose" and most businesses are dancing as fast as they can to merely keep up, there may be trouble ahead.

Small companies must use everything they can to succeed. In his recent book, *The Strategy Paradox*, Michael Raynor says this well:

> The external environment in which we find ourselves is very uncertain, where changes in regulations, the economy, competitors' behavior, customer preferences or new or disruptive technologies could each, or in combination, dramatically change the operating landscape. The ability to take bold action with urgency, while maintaining strategic flexibility has never been more important.

## BOOSTING PROFITS NOW

*Run Your Business Like a Fortune 100* is your tool chest for moving up the business elevator of prosperity. As an entrepreneur, your goal is to boost profits now. You do this by making strategic decisions that keep you focused on *only* your highest priorities with the biggest returns on investment.

You'll discover how to do this with the seven PROFITS principles as I introduce you to my world. I reveal how you, an ambitious entrepreneur, can apply Fortune 100 best practices and quickly boost your profits now. Although a variety of principles may help promote your business success, many entrepreneurs find these seven PROFITS principles to be the *80 percent factors*; that is, they are the solid foundation you need for running a profitable, well-integrated business. The other 20 percent of your success comes from what your company contributes uniquely to your customers. These principles will help you focus your thinking, manage more effectively, and operate your small or medium-sized company with greater efficiency. This includes knowing the warning signs of possible problems common in smaller companies.

PROFITS is *not* a framework or model. It is a convenient reminder of seven principles you should follow when making decisions about activities or actions designed to increase your profitability. Though they are simple to memorize, you may find the principles challenging to apply. For this reason, I provide numerous examples of companies that vary in size, industry, and location that use the principles successfully. You will soon see that you *can* run your business like a Fortune 100—without the complexity, bureaucracy, or expense.

**P**   *Position Only for Growth*

**R**   *Reality*

**O**   *Obtain Vital Information*

**F**   *Flexibility*

**I**   *Integration*

**T**   *Test and Revise*

**S**   *Steering the Company*

The first principle, *Position Only for Growth*, refers to profitability, expansion or other measures that define success in your industry. This principle applies to both profit-making and non-profit organizations that are committed to growth. As you apply this principle, *Position Only for Growth*, you gain clarity about your business and consistency in how you evaluate possible directions for moving forward.

*Reality*, which I define as a focus on what is happening *today*, concentrates on difficult issues caused by the emergence of global competitors and disruptive changes that can occur in any industry. Examples show you how recognizing and facing critical issues can save a business under siege. By remaining alert to potential difficulties and aware of all your options, you can avoid traps and anticipate future threats.

*Obtain Vital Information* reminds us that although we need data (and many of us love all the data we can get), many times we have too much of a good thing. You will meet entrepreneurs like yourself who learned how to gather and sort the right amount of the right information to gain knowledge about their customers and minimize risk. As you practice this principle, you will learn how to recognize and manage the valuable information that is most pertinent to your customers.

*Flexibility* focuses on the ability to adapt and shift gears without forfeiting your purpose and mission. The companies showcased learned to develop flexibility within structured processes that inspired greater creativity and enhanced their customer solutions. As you apply this principle, you will broaden your ability to provide customers with innovative approaches for expanding their businesses—along with your profits.

*Integration*, the linking of all aspects of your business, provides an opportunity to analyze your entire business in the context of a jigsaw puzzle. The examples demonstrate a lockstep approach to align and foster congruency within your company. Practicing this principle will guide you in curtailing unnecessary activities, adding cohesiveness to your projects, and accelerating your profitability.

The *Test and Revise* principle refers to the scope of your business and the strategies you have in place. Nothing zaps a company's energy like scope creep, which denotes the tendency companies have to slowly but surely take on projects tangential to their purpose. The inevitable result is loss of focus. The examples demonstrate how you can maintain your range of control when you modify your strategy based on changing customer requests. You will learn practices to stay within cost, time, and process constraints as you purposefully flex in the middle of a project.

*Steering the Company* is the principle defined by the effective and efficient interaction of people working in a collaborative, unified and organized business environment. These interactions are the key to ensuring the coordination of all aspects of your company. This includes your company's culture and ways to identify the dysfunctional behaviors that impede flexibility, adaptability to change, and effective relationships. The small and medium-sized businesses highlighted apply best practices of Fortune 100 companies that excel in defining clear roles, responsibilities, and accountabilities. Your application of this principle will inspire you to consider and apply specific actions to create a motivated and aligned organization of people you can rely on to heighten trust in relationships throughout the company and with your customers.

In Part II of this book, we build on the foundation of the seven principles with the tool kit for *Run Your Business Like a Fortune 100*. These tools are the means for analyzing your business within the context of your market, your competitors, and your customers. Knowing your ideal customer profile, you avoid the anxiety that comes with uncertainty and the fear of turning a customer away. Your company will have the tools for achieving profitability and for meeting your needs and your customers' needs with a relaxed confidence and aplomb.

The Business Reality Change Model raises the bar for peak performance in the small and medium-sized company. This model employs a systematic, structured yet flexible approach for evaluating your business and builds upon all seven PROFITS principles. You will learn the critical thinking underlying the Business Reality Change Model and comprehend how a business of any size utilizes the model in the business planning process. The model provides you with specific action steps for developing, monitoring, and reviewing goals.

The tools for performance and talent management take the mystique out of complicated people processes and leadership. The corporate complexities of people processes, including employee competency designs, performance management, employee/leadership development, and succession planning, become straightforward and easy to understand. In performance and talent management, small and medium-sized businesses can succeed in ways that are more difficult for larger enterprises. The combination of all these tools will significantly increase your company's efficiency, upgrade your talent pool, and enhance customer relationships.

The Consultative Dialogue (CD) is the tool for promoting continuous improvement and communication throughout your business. Dialogues include performance reviews, talent reviews, weekly updates, quarterly strategic reviews, and ongoing best-selling products updates. As you examine several examples of companies like your own, you will learn how to hone these tools and view them as critical elements of your business. This is important because when you have essential information about your company within your grasp at all times, your business acumen and performance soar.

*What to Do Right Now!*, the book's finale, answers the question, "*What can I do at this very moment—right now?*"

After learning the seven PROFITS principles and the tools for boosting profits, how can you advance your business from *just* being successful to becoming a model of peak profitability? Your goal as the book draws to a close centers on a single powerful idea: *Invest in transforming changes to the business that are both high priority and provide a high return on investment.*

What actions can you implement to sustain growth and increase profitability? The seven principles (PROFITS) and the tools presented in *Run Your Business Like a Fortune 100* challenge you to learn about the best practices of large company processes and how to use them in your successful small or medium-sized business. Get ready to ask yourself penetrating questions, reading examples of many companies that learned important lessons on their journey to success, and then, as the saying goes, "take what you like and leave the rest."

# CHAPTER 2

# PROFITS

*It is a peaceful thing to be one succeeding.*

—Gertrude Stein

Melanie Norris, CEO of Environmental Inc., and I are at a restaurant in St. Moritz. Her concerns about running her $35 million company sound familiar. As we start eating the truffle pizza just delivered by the waiter, she tells me, "I have a new competitor in our critical East Asian market that's really got me worried. As you know, we have two subsidiaries. One of them, GreenSoap Company with its best-selling commercial detergent line, GreenSoap, is in jeopardy and I don't have resources right now to get something new to market fast enough to head them off."

"Please listen," I interject. "You have a successful business. You recently sold a small company. You're familiar with some of the best practices of the Fortune 100 companies because you've already implemented many of them. What do you think might happen if you integrated the many different functions of your business? Do you suppose it might enable you to discover solutions you don't see right now?"

Melanie wonders if it might be true.

She continues, "I understand marketing and finance. I understand my products, and I know my customers. I can assemble the pieces, but I'm not sure how to get every function operating effectively together and at the same time! Besides, with a team of 38, I have only a few in each function and most are out in the field with customers."

I ask Melanie if she can think of how the company's size might be advantageous in a situation like this, in which the business needs more resources just to stay even.

"Well, there's no bureaucracy to slow us down," she volunteers.

"That's right," I say. "You can sit together in a room, share important information, collaborate, and formulate decisions. If you were part of a larger enterprise, it would be more difficult to gather information and take timely action."

"That's true," Melanie agrees. "Still, there's no road map for companies like mine. I don't have the people or the money to drive big strategies and processes that make larger companies successful."

She continues, "Sometimes my company seems chaotic. The day-to-day organization doesn't function as smoothly as I would like. We don't have enough people to deal with the tasks and challenges requiring attention. Everyone is caught up in his or her own activities and we usually are in crisis mode anytime we get together. Our product people complain that the salespeople are making unrealistic promises that their teams now have to deliver on. Of course, the finance group wants more cost cuts. Eventually we compromise, but making decisions is painful for us, and we probably make more than our share of mistakes. I know it's not a good way to operate."

## WHY IS THIS CONVERSATION IMPORTANT?

You may be able to relate to Melanie. She wants to enjoy the successes of her profitable environmentally friendly products company. She is a leader in her field and sophisticated in many business practices. Yet to Melanie, the business seems unorganized, fragmented, and sometimes on the brink of disaster. Every new competitor emerges as a possible threat, and Melanie reacts from a crisis perspective. Time is lost and money wasted until everyone finally agrees on a course of action for coping with the impending issue. Constantly having to respond defensively can exhaust your hardiest workers and further inhibit productivity.

Melanie finds it difficult to react differently. Why? This is probably because it is hard to break well-set patterns in a business. And the thought of replacing familiar behaviors with new ways of responding is daunting.

Later chapters offer questions and suggest solutions that can help both Melanie and you make sure you prepare for the unexpected.

## WHY THE PROFITS PRINCIPLES?

When you *Run Your Business Like a Fortune 100*, you derive most benefit from the *linkage* of PROFITS principles, not just their stand-alone effects. Often when we implement business practices that we hear about, we simply patch these onto existing processes. Though these one-off efforts may appear to have their intended effect, *it is difficult to measure their impact on the company as a whole.*

For example, a financial planner at Amsen Insurers attends a seminar and learns to sell a new product for the company—an insurance annuity plan. Upon returning from the seminar, she spends a day developing a plan for marketing the product. What she does *not* do is ask some crucial questions *before* she begins her work:

- Do annuity products fit my overall strategy and leverage my existing resources and strengths?
- What support will I need to integrate this product with the rest of my line?
- Will other financial planners be able to sell this effectively?

- Can the company cross-sell this product with other products?

In her excitement to generate new, profitable sales, our financial planner is about to rush the annuity to market without understanding the full potential business impact. By asking the right questions first, she can set her business on a correct course for success—or make an informed decision to delay the product or not add it at all.

Gary offers us another example. As a creative marketer, he is more inclined to design an elegant and nuanced marketing plan than a detailed project plan and budget. It is only after he begins implementing the plan that he realizes the company must forgo other lucrative opportunities and put added pressure on manufacturing in order to roll out his plan.

Actions create reactions that cascade throughout the company. If you execute one action here, it creates stress elsewhere. You will not always recognize when it happens, because sometimes the results of these actions are not apparent right away. You may be able to relate to these examples by asking the following questions:

- When has your company implemented a successful initiative only to later find that other areas of the business are negatively impacted?
- How did you alleviate the stress this caused?

PROFITS is a comprehensive set of principles for boosting your company to greater profits and sustainable growth. I've applied these principles with many companies to guide and ensure quality assurance.

By following these principles, you always have the basic functions of your business working together toward common goals. This frees you to concentrate all of your time on what makes your business unique. You can then be more focused and effective in determining what is most important and beneficial for your business. You can unclutter your brain and think about the many ideas you may not have the time to reflect on today.

You will discover which concerns about competitors, market conditions, internal conditions, and daily occurrences present serious challenges. *Unfortunately, many entrepreneurs get discouraged and believe further growth eludes them because their markets are mature and their industries oversaturated.* As you learn to work with the seven principles, you begin to view your company and its future from a different perspective. You may reconfigure your business objectives and find new markets to explore. The key task is to integrate your business and see it complete with moving parts. PROFITS helps you *appreciate how the whole is bigger than the sum of its parts.*

## FROM THE FORTUNE 100 TO YOUR SMALL OR MEDIUM-SIZED COMPANY

*Run Your Business Like a Fortune 100* includes cases and examples of small and medium-sized businesses that face many of the same challenges as you. By use of these cases and examples, you will see how the PROFITS principles can help any company navigate to sustainable profit growth—like many Fortune 100 companies.

The PROFITS principles incorporate all the important elements that a small or medium-sized company requires to run effectively. This is also true for very small companies that may not have established specific functions common to larger companies. For example, in a five-person firm, one person may have responsibility for both operations and human resources. This often means that one of those functions suffers as the individual focuses his or her strengths in the other area. Thus, the PROFITS principles are a reminder to be thorough.

The PROFITS principles also remind you to link your strategy to the *entire* company. Strategic integration is probably the most important element for successful Fortune 100 companies. They spend millions of dollars on consultants to help them keep their diverse businesses aligned. Although Fortune 100 companies can invest in developing strategic directives, a small or medium-sized company can develop and implement a strategic directive faster, with less expense, and with greater awareness of subtle market changes because it is smaller. *The challenge to smaller companies is believing that this ongoing focus on linkages is worthwhile.*

## WHAT IS PROFITS?

**P** *Position Only for Growth*

**R** *Reality*

**O** *Obtain Vital Information*

**F** *Flexibility*

**I** *Integration*

**T** *Test and Revise*

**S** *Steering the Company*

### Position Only for Growth

For our purposes, growth is profitability, expansion, or other ways you may define success in your industry. When you *Position Only for Growth*, any change you make keeps you focused on sustainable profitability.

Accounting, Inc. is a company that *positioned only for growth* and remained focused when failure seemed possible. Damian is CEO of this Miami accounting practice, a profitable $40 million business with 55 employees that caters to wealthy South American businesspeople in South Florida. Damian told me his story:

"Recently, one of my clients suggested that I offer 'quick turnaround' accounting services to larger firms in South and Central America. I would be the outsourcing partner for accounting support. That seemed great. My employees are technically competent and enjoy challenges."

Damian continued relating his experience: "For the next six months, I put the word out that Accounting, Inc. could be the new provider of choice for outsourced accounting services in South and Central America as we developed marketing collateral, networked intensely, and acquired three clients. A few months later, the problems began. Clients started to complain about my staff, and the feedback went something like this: 'They are difficult to work with. They are slow. They don't understand my business. They aren't doing what we contracted for.'"

Following this feedback, Damian remained focused as he searched for specific information about what went wrong. Quickly he realized that his staff needed training in South and Central American culture, which, not surprisingly, differed from Miami's. Damian also found that his employees required assistance in understanding the changes within Accounting, Inc.

Damian met with his employees, articulating the goals and results expected of the new venture. Work teams for each customer spent time learning their customer's business needs and wants. Damian invited an expert to speak to his team about the pros and cons of outsourcing.

A few months later, Accounting, Inc. began to see the fruits of its work. Customers made referrals to other customers and spoke positively about Accounting, Inc.'s staff. Employees enjoyed interacting more intimately within their customer's businesses.

## Reality

*Reality* may seem simple and obvious, yet it is often difficult to put into practice. *Reality*, as a PROFITS principle, means sharpening your focus to what is happening *today*. *Reality* is about challenging perceptions and assumptions.

Here are questions for you to consider. What situations are difficult for you to face realistically? How will seeing the situation more clearly affect the day-to-day operation of your business?

Damian of Accounting, Inc. confronted a difficult *reality*. He committed to a new business, one that he thought would be straightforward to implement. When it became clear that his new business initiative for outsourcing his services in South and Central America was failing, Damian and I spoke.

He said, "Initially, I thought outsourcing would be simple, producing a profitable revenue stream, resulting in satisfied customers, and also generate greater challenge and satisfaction for my staff. When it became evident that the company required major changes to accommodate this new line of business, even I had some resistance to making it happen. Although we had the necessary capital for the changes, the obstacles appeared insurmountable."

At this point, many businesspeople become discouraged, cut their losses, or become overly aggressive, even looking for blame in all the wrong places, including their staff and business partners. The other option is to do what Damian did. He accepted *reality*, both acknowledging the problem *and* staying the course.

Damian knew that the outsourcing project would offer his customers innovative approaches for expanding their businesses. It would also create excitement and challenge within Accounting, Inc. In Damian's mind, it was the ideal way to *position for growth*.

As Damian assessed the *reality* of the changes he needed to make, he decided to stay *positioned for growth*. Once he committed to the change wholeheartedly, the *reality* of the obstacles did not seem as overwhelming. He did what he needed to do to make the new venture a success.

### Obtain Vital Information

The PROFITS principle, *Obtain Vital Information*, reminds us that although we need to be informed about our business and our industry, many times we find too much data. Unless the data is digested, it is not particularly useful. When you can use important facts for enhancing knowledge of your customers and ways of relating to them, then you have useful information.

The sheer volume of data available to us is mind-boggling. Some of it is useful, but unnecessary, distracting data is overwhelming. The essence of this principle, *Obtain Vital Information*, is for us to develop skills for differentiating and processing information that is mission critical or potentially useful for the future. Finding the best information for your business varies depending on your industry. This principle reminds you to clarify what you want to know and to be decisive in selecting those areas that address your business priorities. What information do you require to clarify the most important questions you need to resolve?

Jeff, Mary, and Carl own Energizer Fitness, a $1.5 million fitness club franchise, headquartered in Atlanta, appealing to clientele who do not want to pay for the frills offered by more upscale area clubs and spas.

The owners recently purchased market research and found the data insignificant. Carl concluded that it would not help him market the club better because it was limited to statistics about competitive clubs across the country in the same price range as Energizer Fitness. Mary, in contrast, expected to receive data revealing their customers' profiles, including information about their activities and interests, such as entertainment and shopping preferences. Jeff was looking for salary and share of wallet data on how much this segment spent on luxuries. Carl was surprised to hear his colleagues' responses to the data. He had assumed that all three of them wanted the same information when they contracted with the market research company. This difference of opinion and focus was a revelation to him.

I asked the owners for the instructions they had given to the market research firm. Jeff said, "I asked them to provide us with data about comparable markets for health clubs." In *reality*, the market research firm complied with Jeff's request.

This common scenario can be an important learning experience. One of the best ways to *obtain the vital information* you need is to ask your customers directly. You may still want to retain the services of a market research firm for its special expertise and access to relevant data. However, if you do choose to outsource research, it is important to spell out your goals and make your request clearly. Do you want only data or the interpretation of the data that is specific for your industry and/or company? Document the information you expect in writing to ensure that all parties have the same understanding of your request. Communication is essential to detemining the results you obtain.

*Obtain Vital Information* is one of the seven principles because it serves as a reminder to prioritize the information you require to operate your business effectively *before* you begin exploring the databases, reading materials, and the other resources you commonly use for finding the information that is essential for your business today.

## Flexibility

Can you adapt and shift gears in your daily tactics and processes without sacrificing your purpose and mission? Ironically, the principle *Flexibility* requires that you have both strategic and operational structures in place.

Once you *position your business for growth* and establish the critical parameters, you can be *flexible*, creative, guided by clear goals, and positioned to adapt to any curve life throws you. Most of us are able to go with the flow once we are certain about what we want to achieve and where to go.

*Flexibility* is one of the PROFITS principles because being nimble challenges us to question our resistance toward change. If your positioning is correct and you have a clear strategy for achieving your goals, then moving forward can be effortless. If you find yourself resisting and procrastinating, now is the time to shake off reluctance and investigate further to find the obstacles that appear when major change is required. Small changes are usually easier to accept.

Melanie, CEO of Environmental Inc., found that GreenSoap Company was facing growing global competition and disruptive industry changes. She told her colleagues of her concern about a new competitor's product extension that was competing with her best-selling detergent line.

Her competitor, the Green Grocer Company, sold both detergent and softener in one package, underselling Melanie in the category, even though Melanie believed she produced the superior product. Melanie knew she had to take an entirely new approach to counteract the competitor's move. A product extension or copycat defense would not work. Exercising the principle of *Flexibility*, Melanie *realistically* evaluated her company and the capabilities of her people.

Because of Melanie's commitment to *flexible* thinking, she was able to create a new approach to her market segmentation and rally her marketing and manufacturing teams to design new packaging targeted to this new segment. Melanie looked at the facts, and as she faced the *reality* of her situation, she looked for areas of *flexibility* within her company. As a result, she made smart and quick decisions to *position for growth* and increased both market share and profitability. Melanie's *flexibility* enabled her to exploit an opportunity she could not anticipate. She adapted by remembering to think with *flexibility*, rather than reacting immediately.

*Flexibility* is the PROFITS principle that focuses our business parameters and expands our creativity. In the example, Melanie already had her business in good order when faced with a major challenge. She knew she could rely on her marketing staff and the product's manufacturer because they shared her own commitment to creativity and *flexibility*. When your business is under duress, the *Flexibility* principle challenges you to test its limits and your own tolerance for change. Your limitations all come out of hiding when the unpredictable occurs, and it is *Flexibility*, in combination with the other principles, that ensures your business will ride out any threat and continue to thrive.

### Integration

Every element of your business is interconnected. You spend a great deal of time and effort improving your internal processes, but how much do you invest in making sure that all your systems and processes work well together? Do you notice any parts that do not belong with the rest?

*Integration* creates the whole that is bigger than the sum of its parts. It adds cohesiveness and consistency to your business. Work flows from one function to the next seamlessly. Each of your goals makes sense vis-à-vis every other goal. Your business tells a wonderful story for your customers and employees.

In the preceding chapter, you read that the owners of the party supplies distributing company Sky High adapted Fortune 100 best practices after deciding that minor changes would have little impact on profits. After acknowledging the *reality* that these changes would not work, co-owners Judy and Mark determined to increase their profits and integrated Fortune 100 best practices within their existing processes.

Sky High *repositioned for growth*, adjusting its strategy to the *vital information* discovered about the needs of their customers' customers. This resulted in resegmenting the business. Judy and Mark modified the key objectives related to pricing and vendor practices. They also revised Sky High's employee performance system, shifting the rewards and tailoring incentives to coincide with the new growth goals. Instead of hiring an expensive consulting company to restructure their people system, they modified it themselves. (You, too, will learn how to do this in Chapter 11, *People Processes*.) Then they designed new accountability mechanisms, which they also implemented without outside assistance. All they did was tweak their processes in a few places, adopt a handful of Fortune 100 best practices, and then . . . *integrate, integrate, integrate* every step of the way.

The company's sales volume increased by 5 percent between 2007 and 2009, while profits skyrocketed from $2.6 million to $5 million. Sky High attributed the whopping $2.4 million increase to adapting and *integrating* large corporate best practices into its existing processes.

In our earlier example describing the *Reality* principle, the CEO of Accounting, Inc. faced similar issues. Damian's new outsourcing business in South and Central America needed to *integrate* with the Miami accounting business since the entire company shared knowledge, people, and information resources. After some initial problems, Damian *integrated* the company, in part, by conducting frequent employee information-sharing sessions that focused on company goals and successes. He also provided training to educate employees about outsourcing. This *integration* was the foundation for the cohesive, consistent business that Accounting, Inc. currently enjoys.

## Test and Revise

The *Test and Revise* principle is a reminder that your business and your market are constantly changing, so you must remain alert and be prepared to adapt quickly to survive. Many business owners judge these course corrections as minor because they believe their strategy is good. However, after a few nips and tucks, entrepreneurs often allow scope creep to lead them astray. Slowly adding projects that are tangential to your business leads to a patchwork of non-mission-critical projects that do little more than distract you and zap your energy. You attempt to keep up with all the demands on your business and begin to lose focus. Many times this inhibits the *integration* we talked about earlier. One change leads to another, and their effects on your business are different than you might anticipate. Strategy no longer fits with goals. Activities seem unrelated to what you want to achieve. The complexities of rearranging current projects and keeping up with the future pipeline are stressful.

The following illustration of this principle comes from a large corporation, typically known for its best practices. Even well-respected large companies are not immune to difficulties.

In the late 1990s, one of the world's largest banks, headquartered in New York City, attempted to coordinate more than 100 legacy computer systems across the globe. As each business unit attempted to create new software and integrate into the global network, it seemed the process would never end. Each business unit included countries throughout the world that required different specifications. Adding to the confusion were the scores of consultants assigned to various businesses. Each consultant claimed to have the answers. Some units networked into customer and supplier companies that were incompatible with the bank's mainframe. Adjustments to additional information occurred on a daily basis. As you might imagine, the scope creep became astounding. Ten years later, many of these systems are still not *integrated*.

Frequently this lack of *integration* occurs when one area of a business hires a consultant without the knowledge of other divisions in the company. For example, the supply chain logistics gets fixed but the sales strategy remains the same. R&X Construction created an alliance with a new distributor in Kalamazoo, Michigan, to shorten deliveries of cement block from one week to three days. The initial *plan for growth* was to partner with a new distributor, thereby increasing sales of cement block in Michigan via greater delivery efficiency to customers. Yet the sales representatives were out of the loop.

It took four months for the CEO to acknowledge that the sales force needed to meet with the distributor and for supply chain logistics to strategize with the manufacturer to keep enough of the product available for customers.

This is what happens when a company lacks *integration* between its functions. The CEO did *test and revise* his plan when he realized there was a problem. Thus, *Test and Revise* is one of the seven PROFITS principles. It alerts you to the necessary course corrections.

## Steering the Company

Although you are responsible for your business, your success depends on other people you can rely on.

*Steering the Company* is the principle that makes or breaks your business. Your products and services may be profitable, yet without *Steering the Company*, it is unlikely that you will sustain profits for the long term.

*Steering the Company* is the effective and efficient interaction of people working in a collaborative, unified, and organized business environment. Many times, business units of large companies operate like small or medium-sized businesses; and the lessons learned are the same for both types of companies.

The next case looks at a business unit in a large bank. The unit is responsible for the truck and vehicle leasing business. It employs 150 people and has annual revenues of $60 million. The unit is comprised of both contracts and mortgage departments.

There was animosity between the two groups, and the directors assumed they had a crop of bad apples. The more people talked about their dissatisfaction, the more apparent it became that many of their roles and responsibilities overlapped and caused friction regarding the final accountability for results. Was the person who negotiated the lease the one responsible for the contract completion? Who was responsible for obtaining vital information from the customer? Who was responsible for forwarding information? Who followed up with the customer?

The following was the approach suggested. Managers and staff of the contracts and mortgage areas met and together defined every role, responsibility, and final accountability, with assignments for each person. Although this took a while, it was time well spent.

It was evident that problems had been arising because almost everyone involved was taking more than their share of responsibility, and people were tripping over one another. Some people assumed others did not trust them to do their job effectively and were "taking over." Others were supposedly doing more than their share to "look good" to management. It was a comedy of errors, although no one was laughing.

Within a week, the unit was able to process 40 percent more contracts and mortgages than previously, and in less than one month efficiency was 200 percent higher than it had been prior to this exercise.

When a company is profitable, it is especially difficult to rationalize changing what appears to work. The notion "if it ain't broke, don't fix it" reigns. PROFITS can create a sense of urgency in an otherwise complacent business. Using these specific principles as the essential criteria for effective functioning, the small and medium-sized business now has an urgency that energizes a business into action. In my experience, this sense of urgency is much easier to communicate in smaller companies than in large ones.

Finally, PROFITS can jump-start your company to greater awareness for emphasizing performance expectations, particularly those associated with accountability, shared decision making, and measurement. This is of critical importance if you aspire to become a fully integrated company. The PROFITS principles ensure congruence throughout your company. Whether stated or implied, rewarded goals are the goals people achieve most often. Performance systems that measure goal attainment generally take years to develop in Fortune 100 companies, but can be designed and implemented quickly in your smaller business. Chapter 11 will show you how to do just that!

The following seven chapters present detail, additional examples, key issues, and key takeaways for smaller companies for each of the seven PROFITS principles.

## SUMMARY

The key takeaway of this chapter is the insight that the same foundational principles that result in a profitable Fortune 100 company also work to ensure profitability for your small or medium-sized business.

A discussion about why you can draw upon the PROFITS principles for the most important best practices for companies of all sizes followed. This discourse included varied examples, defining each of the seven principles: *P—Position Only for Growth*; *R—Reality*; *O—Obtain Vital Information*; *F—Flexibility*; *I—Integration*; *T—Test and Revise*; *S—Steering the Company*.

## QUESTIONS FOR YOUR BUSINESS PROFITS

Applying new ideas and actions to your business is good practice for making the knowledge real and meaningful. As you begin your journey through the PROFITS principles, it will be beneficial for you to think about the following three key questions and address those that may be useful for your business.

1. *What do I want to accomplish?*
2. *What is the current state of my business?*
3. *What is required for my company to become more profitable?*

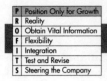

| P | Position Only for Growth |
|---|---|
| R | Reality |
| O | Obtain Vital Information |
| F | Flexibility |
| I | Integration |
| T | Test and Revise |
| S | Steering the Company |

# CHAPTER 3

# Position Only for Growth

*Make your product easier to buy than
your competition, or you will find your
customers buying from them, not you.*

—Mark Cuban, Dallas Mavericks

A mong the seven principles, one stands out as a force that
launches a whole cascade of actions for the other six. *Position Only for Growth* is the lead PROFITS principle and the key
to success.

*Position Only for Growth* is essential to growing any business, and it helps create opportunities for sustaining your
profitable growth. Though these may not strike you as new
ideas, keep the following key points in mind as you think about
this principle. They provide focus, context, and actions to take
when you think about *Position Only for Growth*.

- *Review financial performance*
- *Know your customers and their customers*
- *Assess internal systems*

- *Adapt quickly to competitive shifts*
- *Generate priorities*

The following discussion among three conference panelists is important because it highlights some of the current and future challenges and opportunities facing entrepreneurs who are grappling with *Position Only for Growth* in a competitive marketplace.

*Setting: Small and Medium-Sized Business Panel—Athens, Greece*

*Participants on Panel:*

> *Sean Meyer, CEO, Skeeter Footwear Company, $80 million annual revenues, manufacturer of moderate-price-point footwear, selling to upscale stores such as Bloomingdale's, Burdines, and Saks Fifth Avenue*

> *Jennifer Corbin, CEO, CopperPlumbing, $50 million annual revenues, manufacturer of copper piping for water supply lines, heating, and air-conditioning, with six plants in the United States*

> *Cameron Hernandez, CEO, Medical Imaging Inc., $25 million annual revenues, developer of a Web-based technology platform and database for analyzing high-resolution medical imaging equipment*

The session starts with the moderator questioning the participants about the challenges of profitable growth in today's economy.

Sean says, "No matter how we define growth for our business, the market is the most influential consideration. Look at energy and steel prices today."

Jennifer agrees and adds that whenever costs of raw materials increase, many companies restructure, cut expenses, and ultimately skimp on quality, resulting in lower long-term profitability. "My business is challenged with this right now. CopperPlumbing is a product-focused company in a world of competing products like our own. Though our revenues are increasing, our profits are dwindling. I'm afraid we're becoming a high-volume, low-cost commodity."

The moderator then asks the panelists to talk about the importance of business positioning during these challenging times.

Cameron tells his story: "We had problems similar to Jennifer's a few years ago when imaging equipment manufacturers followed us into providing Web-based analysis tools that worked only on their machines. This led to an erosion of profits we'd enjoyed as a first mover. I thought long and hard about my customers and my competition, realizing that I had to focus on future trends. I saw that some customers fell prey to manufacturers' claims that their own software would provide superior results since it was designed specifically for the imaging equipment in which they'd already invested.

"Then it hit me," he continued. "This was a desperate effort by some manufacturers not to be left out of the market that had begun to move rapidly to Web-based image analysis and verification. We had an edge since our entire business is application development and not hardware manufacturing. My solution was to strike strategic alliances with innovative manufacturers in Asia and Europe and begin bundling our application with their machines. At the same time, we assigned a development group to revise our tools so that we could provide the most comprehensive data and most accurate results, regardless of the equipment. Innovation, in my humble opinion, is the only road to profits—create or partner, then market and sell the new and different. Every product runs the risk of becoming a commodity when your strategy is to lower prices to beat the competition."

Jennifer says she would have to change her business model completely, from being product driven to being market driven. "That would be innovation for us. I do have to face reality. One of my best employees joined a competitor that outsources some of its production and other supply chain areas. Outsourcing could work for us in some areas, too. I have to admit that I don't think much about innovation."

Sean also agrees about the importance of innovation. His strategic positioning is to bring his moderate-priced footwear into high-end stores and to attract younger women with limited incomes who love to shop in these stores. This is profitable for Skeeter Footwear. Sean says, "The biggest threat to Skeeter is to be the seller of just another midpriced shoe in discount marts and price clubs—cutting prices and becoming a commodity. Right now, I believe our model is unique."

The morning continues with issues of funding and finances. Jennifer's company, CopperPlumbing, uses bank credit lines, while Sean puts his profits back into the business for product development and innovation. Cameron's company is funded by venture capitalists.

"Recently I learned," says Cameron, "that my current investors don't want to see unrestrained growth because it could actually diminish their overall portfolio returns. If my company requires too much attention because it operates differently from other companies in the portfolio, then the economy of scale for the portfolio may decrease.

"Then there's the issue of whether to reinvest some of my profits to grow the business. This gives investors angst, because it's more risk for them. The revenues they counted on may be reduced and reinvested into longer-range projects. A company like ours that was early to market and that has been quick to innovate depends on investors who share our vision that our products represent the future of health care. Investors who rely on old business models are not as good a fit for us as we seek additional funding. Some venture capitalists prefer to work with start-ups in order to avoid these complexities, even if a company is profitable. I have ideas about increasing profitability, but some investors I've spoken with have conflicting standards and it's their money. My experience with investors to date has been that their long- and short-term views of growth are very different. Who would have thought?"

## WHY IS THIS CONVERSATION IMPORTANT FOR YOU?

The preceding conversation emphasizes the key issues that entrepreneurs consider everywhere around the globe when they ask themselves: How can I position my company for sustainable growth? The balance between innovative customer solutions, funding sources, cutting costs, and keeping long- and short-term goals aligned is tricky business, yet magic tricks and sleight of hand do not work over the long haul.

Your company may have cash for reinvestment or funding provided by relatives, banks, private equity funds, angels, or venture capitalists. Your business may also be a not-for-profit. Of course, you want your business to contribute to society; yet to remain profitable and grow, every company must generate revenues. This is why the PROFITS principle, *position your company only for sustainable growth* is so important. This does not mean you have to get bigger and bigger. Think of it this way: If your goal is to stay in business for a very long time, your growth must be *sustainable*. This means shutting out any thoughts of growth at any cost or growth for its own sake without regard to the longer-term consequences of growth without restraints. You must show profits or you will eventually be out of business.

Here we define business growth as growth that is sustainable and profitable. This is more than growing market share which may also be an important goal but is far from the whole story. By incorporating Fortune 100 best practices that you learn in this book, you can guide your company to become more profitable, sustainable, and integrated.

## SUSTAINING PROFITABLE GROWTH

I queried clients around the world to define sustainable, profitable growth for their industries. The feedback underscored certain themes across a variety of industries.

### What Does Sustainable, Profitable Growth Mean in Your Industry?

*Ahmed, Pay TV Segment, Bahrain*

Profitable business growth is based on:

- Number of new customers added to the network.
- Retaining existing customers.
- Increasing average revenue per customer.

Ahmed's important growth indexes are revenue growth, network spread (distribution depth/width and client addition), number of new products added at an acceptable revenue level, and growth from new initiatives.

### Shivaji, General Manager in Telecommunications Industry, India

Consider both current and past industry benchmarks when defining profitable growth, using such measures as:

- Market penetration (new partners, customers, territories added).
- Brand recognition.
- Customer preferences.
- Improvement in business processes.
- Customization, enhancements, and policies that occur because of the new opportunities created, generated, and achieved.

### Martin, Entrepreneur, United Arab Emirates

The main criterion for sustainable growth is percentage increase in shareholder value.

### Richard, Entrepreneur Running Companies in Emerging Markets (Russia, Ukraine, and India), San Francisco

Define business growth by comparing return on investment in your industry and sector, and measure it in terms of:

- Innovation in product design, manufacturing, sales, marketing, business process, organizational structures, and/or utilization of new technology.
- Productivity improvement based on a level achievable using fewer resources without compromising quality or customer value.

### Ari, Technology Entrepreneur, Israel

Business equals revenue growth. All company functions support growth, including human resources, manufacturing capacity, and operational excellence. A pre-revenue start-up business plan must show how growth contributes to generating profits quickly.

### Kikan, Venture Capitalist, Africa

Common measures for sustainable growth are:

- Growth of the company's equity.
- Increase of profits/revenues vis-à-vis costs each year.
- Improvement in productivity per capita and yields.
- Increased overall balance sheet growth.
- Reduced costs/losses.
- Expansion of business units/manpower.
- Maximization of market share.
- Customer retention along with an increasing customer base.

As you can see, entrepreneurs employ many variables for measuring growth and profitability. It is important for you to know what the standard metrics are in your industry.

## HOW DO ECONOMISTS DEFINE GROWTH AND PROFITS?

After perusing more than 100 books and business journals to find a consistent definition of growth, the term *sustainable growth* remains an enigma. This is true throughout microeconomics literature and extends to businesses of all shapes and sizes, including private companies and nonprofits. Entrepreneurs, as you read in our global sample of entrepreneurs, each define appropriate characteristics of sustainable growth for their company and their industry. Then they decide whether to invest and expand their business or squeeze out all the profits they can, working with what they have.

According to Nobel Prize–winning economist Joseph Stiglitz, "The cost and availability of funds address one side of the firm's investment decision. The other side is the expected returns of the funded projects. This is growth."

There are also growth matrixes à la McKinsey and the Boston Consulting Group (BCG) that rank companies by relative market share, slotting your company in a box that categorizes it as a star, cash cow, dog, or question mark (GE Matrix). Michael Porter offers strategies to build and analyze your portfolio of products. Each methodology provides information with limitations based on individual company characteristics. Though theories vary, reading some of the strategy books can help you formulate metrics and criteria for your own business. The more holistic your perspective, the more knowledge you have to support important decisions.

## BUSINESS ESSENTIALS

Successful entrepreneurs continually ask themselves the three key questions raised in the last chapter:

1. *What do I want to accomplish?*
2. *What is the current state of my business?*
3. *What is required for my company to become more profitable?*

Answering these questions helps reinforce the vision and purpose of your business in a thorough and comprehensive way. Keeping the answers to these questions in mind as you continue to read this book will help you apply the organizing principles and tools.

## REVIEW FINANCIAL PERFORMANCE

Obviously, the business you run *must be* profitable. Yet, the very reason for your success is the same reason you intuitively know that your company can perform better. As you review your financial performance, the following actions will help boost your profits.

- *Ask penetrating questions*
- *Determine current financial needs*
- *Recognize interrelationships between financial measures*

When you query your financial performance thoroughly, as Sean did in the following example, you discover important clues that affect the future of your business.

## Ask Penetrating Questions

Sean Meyer, CEO of Skeeter Footwear (a panelist in the chapter's opening example) distributes moderate-price-point footwear to boutiques and large retail chains.

As Sean delved into Skeeter Footwear's recent financial performance and company history, he thought he was moving in a positive direction. Skeeter Footwear increased sales by 7 percent in two consecutive years following several years of overall declining sales throughout the athletic shoe sector, due to bad publicity globally about business practices such as child labor. Skeeter's increase was due to supply chain enhancements, particularly in its shipping and trucking routes.

In 1966, when Nike introduced the Tiger Cortez model, a lightweight nylon and suede shoe with a cushioning sole and good support, the world of athletic footwear began to change. The tipping point occurred as the world of physical fitness and sports medicine created footwear categories for individual sports and fashion. Sean's Uncle Lawrence jumped into the fray when he started Skeeter Footwear Company in 1986, as Reebok unseated Nike from its number one position in the United States. In 2000, Sean became CEO of Skeeter Footwear.

As Sean pondered how to position the company, he asked himself the following questions:

- Are profits growing at 10 percent or more annually?
- How did investments/assets contribute to specific areas of profit?
- What other business practices improved profitability? How?

- What did not work and why?
- What percentage of profitability resulted from existing customers? Are these customers segmented into specific tiers?
- What percentage of profitability resulted from new customers? Are these customers segmented into specific tiers?

After Sean reviewed the cold, hard facts, he realized he had to make some difficult decisions. One fact he discovered was that Skeeter's profitability from existing customers decreased over the past year. This both disappointed and encouraged him. Being able to define a tangible problem that he could potentially solve offered hope of turning the situation around. Sean's story illustrates the notion that although many times we believe we know the facts, often we do not have all of the details necessary to inform our decisions.

Although sitting down with the balance sheet, income statements, and cash flow records is tedious, it provides the basic information for solid future financial planning decisions.

## Determine Current Financial Needs

Sean next considered Skeeter's current financial needs before deciding how to proceed. He assessed his expenses for the next few months, which provided the current financial direction—a necessary first step before positioning for a more profitable future.

Reginald Sawyer, owner of gift shop and bookseller Reading Shack, once told me that he is reluctant to review his current financial business records. He is not always sure about his current financial needs since they vary each month. For some of us there is an illusion that not knowing the facts keeps us safe. Unfortunately, not knowing the facts actually prevents us from keeping our company healthy.

Once you know the basic facts and current financial needs for your business, you will want to consider the interrelationships between the financial facts.

### Recognize Interrelationships Between Financial Measures

Knowing these interrelationships will help you understand the financial story line for what is happening in your business. This story line highlights areas of your finances you will want to pay attention to for improving your bottom-line profits.

Your cash position defines your liquid assets—the money you have readily available. Ask yourself: What can I do with more cash to grow my business?

Some companies use available cash to expand strategically. They borrow less money for working capital. What is the current interest rate environment? Does it make more sense for you to borrow money or to trim your expenses now? How much inventory do you carry? How quickly does it turn over? Are you relying on a markdown strategy to sell off older products? Do you know the standards for velocity or inventory turnover within your industry? Is your goal to increase profit margins or to sell the most volume possible, even at a lower price? How do you reconcile market share with your profitability? These are complicated questions.

*Decisions about positioning your business MUST take into account the interrelationships between these financial variables.*

You cannot run a profitable, sustainable business without understanding the relationships between the financial variables. If you do not have a firm understanding of the basics of finance, get educated! If you learn to consider financial interrelationships and sort through their complexities, you will be better able to pinpoint areas of your business for your greatest profitable next steps. Otherwise, you may unknowingly compromise the future growth of your business.

Reginald, the bookstore owner, spent more than double his available assets on Reading Shack's operating expenses when the store resided in an expensive commercial district in Greenwich, Connecticut. A stockroom full of unsold inventory further reduced Reading Shack's profitability. Reginald reluctantly assessed his basic finances. He then explored even deeper, appraising his asset-to-debt ratio, inventory expense, velocity,

**44**

and profit margin. Finally he knew that he had to relocate Reading Shack to a less expensive neighborhood and change his product mix and especially his purchase methods. This was a very difficult decision for him.

As a result of the relocation to Stamford, Connecticut, Reginald positioned his store for growth with a marketing plan and discount strategy. Within three years, Reginald's business changed radically. His strategic approach was to decrease his inventory quantities to conserve cash. He switched to higher-margin gift items, established an alliance with a reputable discount wholesaler, and started purchasing books on the best-seller list faster than other stores in his market area. With operating costs reduced due to his lower rent, Reginald now borrows less, and his profits more than tripled to $600,000 this year.

Let us return to Sean, the CEO of Skeeter Footwear. After analyzing the financial facts and assessing how they relate, Sean identified the supply-and-demand statistics for the footwear industry as best he could. He researched possible customer criteria that helped determine how Skeeter Footwear's products compared to his competitors'. Sean's financial analysis helped him determine his pricing strategy. He also measured his own inventory levels against industry norms, targeted new customers, and modified his positioning within the footwear industry. As larger corporations such as Wal-Mart, Citigroup, and Ford would do when facing similar issues, Sean then evaluated the "share of the customer's wallet" his company could achieve. As a result, he strengthened relationships with his existing clients and reached out to more potential clients using the information he learned.

## KNOW YOUR CUSTOMERS AND THEIR CUSTOMERS

"Know your customers and their customers" is such an overused maxim that most people never think about its complexity.

What's more, your customers today may not be your customers tomorrow. You will benefit from the following strategies as you think about your customers:

- *Build inspiring relationships*
- *Know your company from your customers' perspective*
- *Remember to cross-sell*

As you know, customers are more savvy now than in the past. They have more choices due to the Internet and other efficient distribution channels. Global markets and a "flatter" world have increased customer shopping alternatives. Without overstating the point, you first must know where your customers are, where your potential customers shop and where *their* customers shop. Then, you need to inspire them.

## Build Inspiring Relationships

Citibank understood the value of building inspiring relationships. In 1998, the philosophy was to spend the time developing strong customer rapport. The unwritten rule was not to rush through the selling process. Customer relationship managers frequently visited companies in various industries that might need their products.

For example, Charles, a Vice President in the Global Trade Finance product group, met with a telecommunications customer bimonthly to establish a friendly presence and ask specific questions about its priorities and those of its customers. At the end of the first year, the telecom requested that a Citibank employee spend two full days a month within its business offices. The purpose of this was for Citibank to be available to educate the telecom about the quickly changing market and for the bank and company to work together to design new and better pre- and postsale products and services for customers.

As the relationship evolved, Charles knew that the people at the telecom company trusted him. The next step was for Charles to gain in-depth understanding of its business needs. For Citibank to provide the best solutions, Charles needed to comprehend the company's financial profile (similar to the previous case analyses of Sean and Reginald), and its customers' needs. For example: What were the key drivers, psychologically as well as financially, in their decision-making processes? How did they determine price points?

## Know Your Company from Your Customers' Perspective

What are your customers buying? What is the basis of their choices? How do you measure up to your customer's standards? How do customers perceive your products and the way you operate your business?

From its customers' perspective, what was the telecommunications company selling to its customers? Was it reliability, functionality, security, cool phones, or all of the above? Charles needed to identify this telecommunications customer's purchasing, approval, and decision-making processes. Each time he returned to Citibank after meeting with his client, Charles reviewed what he learned with peers and with colleagues in other departments. With the benefit of this input, Charles expanded his vision of what he could offer his customer. Charles asked the telecom managers about their business strategies, tactical plans, core business processes, performance measurement, and other important metrics. At times, Charles proposed possible changes to this customer's positioning.

As small or medium-sized business entrepreneurs, you can also apply this best practice of understanding what you are truly selling from the customers' perspective to increase your "share of the customer's wallet." It certainly works exceptionally well for Citibank.

When you know your customers and what they spend their "share of wallet" on, you will know what else your customers and their customers want to buy to augment what they recently purchased.

## Remember to Cross-Sell

Cross-selling is a successful approach to use *after* spending significant time building a relationship with your customer. Rather than selling a menu, you integrate your offerings into a seamless package, segmented into vertical customer tiers or bundled into a variety of attractive options. You will also want to create a value proposition—a statement that lets your customers know how you add value for them. And of course, maintaining a level of customer service after the sale is the continuation of the sales process, often leading to more business.

In addition, you need to find out how your customers perceived every person they interfaced with in your company. This feedback is invaluable and will have a direct impact on whether your customer continues doing business with you. This may sound like a lot of work. It is. If you are lucky, you may be able to replicate some of your customer offerings to several customers. Additionally, to cross-sell most effectively, you may find that some of your company's internal systems require modifications.

## ASSESS INTERNAL SYSTEMS

The next consideration that your company can benefit from when you *Position Only for Growth* is an assessment of your internal systems. Sustainable growth relies on optimal day-to-day operations within your company. Though this inner focus will not directly result in greater profitability, it is a prerequisite for operating effectively. There are three key actions to consider for maximizing operations within your internal systems.

- *Increase efficiencies for operating profits*
- *Alleviate customer constraints to working with you*
- *Outsource non-core operating expenditures*

Your internal systems are your tools. Similar to a carpenter, without the right tools, it is difficult to complete your projects with excellence.

### Increase Efficiencies for Operating Profits

Efficiency in internal functioning, in all aspects of your company, increases operating profits. This provides the cash you need to fund other opportunities, both inside and outside your daily operations. You can easily find specific books and articles that provide the know-how for improving each of your internal systems.

## Alleviate Customer Constraints to Working with You

Melanie, CEO of Environmental Inc.,whom you read about in Chapter 2, took steps to assess and enhance most of her internal systems to make it easier for customers to work with her company. These systems included supply chain, human resources, accounting, legal, technology, marketing, sales, and operations. Melanie overhauled accounting, specifically the purchasing, accounts payable, and accounts receivable functions. As a result, her customers obtained faster credit approvals and subsequently paid her sooner. Melanie did not want her own accounting system to be an obstacle for companies doing business with her.

Melanie then leveraged her strength in human resources management by developing best practice areas in people processes. She wanted to position her company far ahead of her competitors by attracting the best people in the industry. Her main competitors had high employee turnover, less evolved compensation/reward systems, and less clarity regarding effective training and development. As a result of the changes she introduced, Melanie is now considered a leader in people processes. She recently spoke at the Society for Human Resource Management national conference, and Environmental Inc. received the award in *GreenWays* trade journal for Best Employee Practices of the Year.

## Outsource Non-Core Operating Expenditures

Melanie outsourced some of her weaker supply chain areas. She hired a logistics firm to scope out the shortest delivery routes on the West Coast and a container company to package shipments overseas. However, she decided to maintain the customer service function within the company so that her employees could interface with their customers directly. As a result of outsourcing the supply chain areas where she had less capability, Melanie can now dedicate more time to Environmental Inc.'s strongest capabilities, which are sales, marketing, and customer service.

Did this added attention to processes take extra time? Yes. However, it allowed Melanie's employees to generalize from both the positive and the negative lessons learned for future projects. Since turnover is now low in her company, these lessons learned became the new norms and expectations within the company's culture.

By contrast, David, CEO of an import/export firm, decided it was too costly to streamline his operations area. He hired a local company to document and pick incoming purchases for distribution to stores, another company in Guatemala to schedule and route packages for global overnight delivery and still another company to provide telemarketing. He was able to eliminate 55 people in the supply chain function. David's company, like Melanie's, continued to provide its own customer service as a way to influence its valuable customer relationships.

Your creativity infinitely expands your available options. First, when you have to evaluate your internal systems, understand how they work together, and then determine your strengths and weaknesses. As a rule, you will want to leverage your strengths and outsource your weaknesses. Leveraging your strengths benefits you because they help you adapt quickly to most competitive shifts.

## ADAPT QUICKLY TO COMPETITIVE SHIFTS

You keep abreast of your industry. You know your customers' expectations. You assess your own internal capabilities continuously. You identify your financial needs for staying profitable. You recognize your strengths and mediocre areas.

With this portfolio of knowledge, you can determine your best moves for adapting quickly to competitive shifts within your market. Consider how to:

- *Distinguish yourself*
- *Expand your thinking about possible competitors*

Competition is a fact. In our flat world, entry of new competitors is easier than in the past. Companies can enter our markets instantly if someone has a good idea, technology know-how, and strong social networks. This challenge is now a reality.

### Distinguish Yourself

Ask yourself right now, How is my company unique? In what ways does my company differentiate from competitors? Where are my vulnerabilities vis-à-vis those of competitors? Do I know who my competitors are?

### Expand Your Thinking About Possible Competitors

During my tenure at Linens-n-Things, the ongoing competitive focus was Bed Bath & Beyond. Our sources at Bed Bath & Beyond told us of their obsessive focus on Linens-n-Things. Although the two were obvious competitors, they were not each other's only competition. Costco, Wal-Mart, and any other store selling towels, sheets, tabletop and glassware products were also the competition. As superstores became one-stop shopping, an emphasis on price points, though still important, began having less impact on those customers who wanted to save time. Those items that were "good enough" for these customers were .... good enough.

When Reginald, CEO of Reading Shack, was still located in high-end Greenwich, Costco's inventory included many of the best sellers that Reginald sold at retail prices. At that time, there were three Costco wholesale stores within 20 minutes of Reading Shack, to the north, south, and west. Customers purchasing their groceries were more than willing to purchase a best-selling book on the tables they passed on their way to the freezer case. Did they enjoy perusing books at Reading Shack, where they could sit on Laura Ashley covered sofas and view books on mahogany shelves? Sure they did. Was it worth the time to find parking on Greenwich Avenue and to schmooze with Reginald? For some people it was. For most, it was a luxury and they did not indulge.

It was easier and less expensive to buy books at Costco where they could also buy milk and eggs.

How are you vulnerable to competitive shifts? Can you anticipate these shifts? Are you following the leaders in your industry and observing how they preserve their profits and market share? Are you visiting their businesses and speaking with their customers? If not, it may be time to do so, as well as to consider and reassess your priorities.

## GENERATE PRIORITIES

Business owners usually begin the year by generating priorities based on customer needs. Then they tend to assess their finances and internal efficiencies. Is there a logical sequence for prioritization? You may consider the following actions as you think about generating priorities:

- *Evolve priorities logically*
- *Create the best customer experience*

### Evolve Priorities Logically

Evolving priorities is a rational process. Though it may seem more natural to base your priorities on your company's capabilities, this may not coincide with what your customers want to buy. When profitability is your goal, your priorities must be those that respond to your customers' needs and to your customers' convenience. Your evolving relationship with your customers will provide the information you need to adapt to their current desires.

At this point the question to ask is, How do I create the best customer experience possible? For this experience, spare no expense. There is nothing more important, including price and functionality, than creating the ideal customer experience.

### Create the Best Customer Experience

People make emotional decisions. Although a great product or service is a must, it is not a good enough reason for a purchase.

**52**

We all make purchase decisions based on how a product reflects on how we feel about ourselves. Does your product or service promise security, being cool, or a reflection of wealth or intelligence? Only after the purchase do we make up a story to support our buying decision. Only then do we talk about the fine quality, great value, artistic design, or durability of the product or service. To be successful, you must supply a story line for your customer that is easy to communicate and compels your customer to buy your product. The following is an example of how Clarisa Shand, CEO of Nantucket Frocks, creates the emotional experience that encourages customers to visit her store frequently and purchase her products often.

Two years ago, Clarisa realized that she was selling prestige and security in addition to lovely apparel. Prior to that time, her sole focus was on importing expensive fabrics from Thailand. Sales were profitable, yet Clarisa sensed she could better define her priorities. As she and her staff learned more about her customers and their needs, Clarisa began to cater to her customers' wish to dress elegantly and be noticed for excellent taste and couture. After Clarisa assessed her financial situation, she developed an investment budget for future growth. She refurbished her shop, embellishing it with natural woods and expensive decor. She hired an interior decorator and purchased authentic artwork.

As Clarisa designed her new shop, she literally became the customer. In the customer role, she wanted her shopping experience to go beyond viewing dresses on a rack. As a result, Clarisa's shop displayed vases of fresh flowers, bowls of Godiva chocolates, and upscale magazines at the registers. When entering the shop, Clarisa offered her customers a crystal goblet of champagne. Nantucket Frocks now carries a limited inventory of one-of-a-kind dresses, and customers flock to Clarisa's exclusive and very profitable shop.

## SUMMARY

*Positioning Only for Growth* results in success when you carefully review your financial performance by asking penetrating questions, determining your current financial needs, and verifying interrelationships between financial measures. You know who your customers and their customers are by building inspiring relationships, understanding your company from your customers' perspective, and remembering to cross-sell.

You assess your internal systems to increase the efficiency of operating profits, to alleviate customer constraints to working with you, and to outsource noncore operating expenditures. You adapt quickly to competitive shifts as you distinguish yourself and expand your view of who your competitors are.

Finally, you generate priorities by evolving them logically and creating the best customer experience in the industry. The examples in this chapter, including Skeeter Footwear, Citibank, Nantucket Frocks, and Reading Shack, demonstrate the benefits for how comprehensive analysis of your business leads to solid business judgment. As you move your company toward a *Position Only for Growth*, you face a large dose of realism.

The next focus is the principle *Reality*. This principle provides the opportunity for you to investigate and to enhance your capacity to cope with situations beyond your control.

## QUESTIONS FOR ASSESSING YOUR BUSINESS PROFITS

- How do you define sustainable growth and profitability for your business?
- What percentage of profitability results from your existing customers? What percentage comes from new customers?
- How do customers perceive your products and your business?
- How does your company operate efficiently? How does it operate inefficiently?
- Can you quickly adapt to competitive shifts?

| P | Position Only for Growth |
|---|---|
| **R** | **Reality** |
| O | Obtain Vital Information |
| F | Flexibility |
| I | Integration |
| T | Test and Revise |
| S | Steering the Company |

# CHAPTER 4

# Reality

*And that's the way it is.*

—Walter Cronkite

You need to have a good grip on *reality* to build a successful business. All your hopes and dreams go for naught if you miss what's happening in the here and now. The *Reality* principle offers you the opportunity to look at these important and common experiences:

- *Facing facts*
- *Responding to disasters*
- *Committing to your business*
- *Dealing with uncertainty*
- *Letting go*

*Reality*, the "R" in PROFITS, invites you to evaluate how your business measures up against its peers and where you fit in the ecosystem. You can dream about tomorrow. You can regret or idealize the past. But ... we live today. Your company is here now. This is the moment for you to determine what you will do next. *Reality* is your friend.

This little story illustrates a company's struggle to face a painful reality. Fortunately, it rallied the courage to move forward and turned a disastrous situation into a projected $100 million revenue business by 2010.

"How did this happen?" implored Cassandra, as she reviewed third quarter financial results for Jonas CD/DVD Inc.

"Peer-to-peer networks," Rafi explained. "People download and share all their music over the Internet. Everybody's grandmother has pirated music on her iPod," he added with disgust.

Jonas CD/DVD is a $25 million social network that targets musicians and their music. Based in the northern suburbs of Los Angeles, Jonas CD/DVD employs five full-time employees and a host of freelancers.

In 1998, the company began as a music retailer of compact discs. It struggled for two years before Jim Burns, CEO, accepted the truth. Downloading music from the Internet was not going away, Napster legislation notwithstanding. If the company did not change direction, it's Power Off.

Jim Burns knew he had to step up to the plate. He reviewed all financial statements for the prior five years with his CFO and investors. They thought long and hard about the viability of the business, reviewing its strengths and weaknesses in current and potential new markets.

Burns, who had a strong background in music production and sales, convinced investors that there was a market for content production and sales of orchestrated sound bites of contemporary music. The business would offer products and production services for every medium.

The team decided to *position for growth* with a strong plan for moving forward. This included major changes in how the company interacted with customers, suppliers, and employees. Jonas CD/DVD formed numerous strategic alliances with companies across various industries and demographic segments. It designed an alluring interactive social networking community, providing compelling content with links to other Internet sites.

With projected revenues of $100 million for 2010 and double that revenue for 2013, Jonas CD/DVD has successfully reached the next necessary step for boosting profits.

## WHAT HAPPENED?

Jonas CD/DVD's management team responded with courage as the company faced facts, responded to adversity, committed to the business, dealt with uncertainty, and knew when it was time to let go of the old business model.

What thoughts drifted through your mind as you read this vignette? Can you recall a time when you too, compelled to deal with complex challenges, stepped up, made difficult decisions and solved a challenging dilemma?

## FACING FACTS

Facing facts is an obvious condition when confronting reality. You may find these four aspects of facing facts beneficial to reflect upon:

- *Recognize your financial situation*
- *Cut through complexity*
- *Satisfy your customers*
- *Be a formidable competitor*

### Recognize Your Financial Situation

A thorough and clear-eyed financial review of your business requires assessing the financial state without taking outside influences into consideration. In other words, it means taking full responsibility for 'what is' without blaming the industry, current events, or any other external forces. A comprehensive financial review is your best barometer of profitability and health. One limitation is that financial facts are lagging indicators. That means your data gauges past performance, and of course you cannot change the past. When recognizing your financial situation, here are a few questions to ask:

- Are you disappointed with your company's current level of performance?
- Are you frustrated because previous efforts to improve your business's performance have not delivered actual improved financial results?
- What is stopping significant improvements in productivity and profitability?
- Do you know your fixed costs? Do you know your variable costs?
- Are you measuring the right factors?

These are questions you personally need to know the answers to at any given time, whether you have the best CFO on your staff or not.

Delving a little deeper into your fixed costs might provide insights. For example, Venator Group, a retail holding company, had a policy for keeping all Foot Locker store expenses at the store level. This included not moving merchandise between locations unless the store's truck was filled to full capacity to save on costs. However, a sales associate calculated that the cost of moving merchandise between stores with the purpose of replenishing an item that was out of stock at another store was actually less costly than losing the sale. He reasoned that an inconvenienced customer who finds an item out of stock may not return to the store and may even complain to other customers. Thus, sometimes an underfilled truck delivering an item to an understocked store would actually make a positive contribution to profits. This associate was able to get to the essence of a complex situation.

## Cut Through Complexity

American International Group (AIG) completed a flurry of merger and acquisition deals in the late 1990s and early 2000s.

**58**

Although the deals appeared lucrative, high costs surfaced as AIG attempted to integrate the cultures of its acquisitions into its own. These efforts focused primarily on technology and human resources systems.

You may benefit by reviewing your alliances and partnerships for hidden and unanticipated costs. What expenses beyond the obvious ones do you bear? Include time with your partners on the telephone, in person, at meals, in transit, and other hidden costs. Are you earning sufficient return on your investment in advertising promotions, marketing, discounts, and other related fees? Other questions you ought to be able to answer are:

- What is your cost of capital?
- Are your margins shrinking or increasing?
- Are your inventories too high or adequate?

Once you have the basic information pertaining to your business, consider some operational indicators that may provide insight. Are you paying overtime frequently to complete orders? If so, is this because due dates are often missed? Do priorities change often? Is it difficult to respond to customer demands? Are there frequent shortages of materials, parts, and/or supplies? Do improvements in one department often come at the expense of others? Do you measure what you do?

As you approach this task, consider yourself a detective. As you address these questions, can you link them to problematic financial issues? Can you find a cause-and-effect connection between some of the variables? Remember, this is not an exercise to place blame on any one functional area. Every problem builds on others and the result is a cascade effect, much like the game of dominoes. The more detail you can recover that tells the story of your business, the easier it is to untangle this complexity and to find solutions.

Jennifer, CEO of CopperPlumbing, a $50 million manufacturer of copper piping (Chapter 3, *Position Only for Growth*), was trying to determine why inventory turnover was low in the fourth quarter for the past three years. As she delved into operations, she discovered that plant managers in the Northeast and Midwest tended to hoard copper supplies because there were shortages in the winter months. As she continued to probe, Jennifer realized that her primary supplier in these regions closed its shops between November and February each year. The inventory problem was not evident earlier because the plants hoarded copper tubing and it appeared to be in stock. CopperPlumbing's previous quarterly results included only bottom-line revenues and not inventory turnover. The origin of the revenue problem now became obvious. Due to this discovery, Jennifer changed suppliers. Together, Jennifer and the new supplier established an average monthly metric for the volume of copper piping required each month. An electronic alert now signals lower or higher purchases as compared to the set average. Current revenues are more stable, and inventory turnover is at an all-time high.

## Satisfy your Customers

It is important to know if you can realistically satisfy your customers. Focusing on this goal will save you effort and frustration. For the time being, ask yourself the following: Do you have an accurate understanding of what customer needs you satisfy? What customer wants can you anticipate for the future? How do you bridge the gap between current and future needs? What are you better at than your competition? How do you know? What can your competition do better than you can? How can you fix this?

## Be a Formidable Competitor

For a few years after Sean Meyer, CEO of Skeeter Footwear, took over the company, he believed he was merely manufacturing and selling midpriced sneakers. Yet, as he thought about his customers and his finances, Sean realized that the history of Skeeter Footwear could be a component of his strategic approach.

# Reality

For decades, retailers enjoyed working with Sean's Uncle Lawrence, who was an ethical, respected, and reliable businessperson. Under Lawrence's tutelage, Skeeter sold high-priced footwear to high-end retail stores and boutiques. When Sean became CEO, he changed the company's strategy of selling high-end footwear and began targeting midprice customers. However, stores like Bloomingdale's and Saks Fifth Avenue continued to carry Skeeter Footwear in their inventory, primarily because of his Uncle Lawrence's reputation.

As Sean began to think more objectively about his customers, he realized that much of his good fortune was due to his Uncle Lawrence, the high-end stores rarely carried brands of midpriced footwear. Yet these stores trusted Skeeter Footwear's quality and management. Though Skeeter's midpriced product line continued to be welcome in stores, Sean realized he was not selling just midpriced footwear. He was selling a high-end image to mid-level tiered customers. Results of an informal survey showed that young women chose to buy their midpriced footwear at high-end stores because it made them feel "glamorous and wealthy." Thus, Skeeter Footwear also sold status and prestige to young female customers. Skeeter advertising included subtle messages targeted to this demographic.

When checking in with his accounts, Sean periodically reminded the management of the high-end stores that he was bringing in young female customers. As a result, customers could now enjoy a shopping experience at the high-end stores even though they currently were unable to purchase much of the higher-priced merchandise at this time in their lives. With more babysitting money or gift certificates in the near term or career advancement in future years, these young women might become long-term customers of the high-end stores and their current positive shopping experience boded well for future purchases. This reality appears to be the result of a puzzle Sean solved that promised future success.

The key takeaway in the Skeeter saga is that the brand became a formidable competitor to high-end shoe manufacturers thanks to its relationship with loyal accounts and these successes *are not easily replicated*. Both Lawrence and Sean recognized the importance of taking right actions as a competitive advantage.

*Facing facts* keeps us grounded in reality. We may not like what we learn, but in the long run this is the only way to stay in business. Sometimes we have to face a reality that is beyond anything we could imagine or control. This is certainly true when we have to cope with disasters.

## RESPONDING TO DISASTERS

Though most of this book focuses on factors we can control, the reality is there are circumstances beyond our control. We learn important lessons for success from how others responded to urgent crises. Those who have overcome disastrous situations cite actions that helped them cope including the ones below.

- *Accept what's inevitable*
- *React for survival*
- *Mobilize quickly*
- *Communicate broadly*

No matter how firmly you believe in taking full responsibility for the direction of your company, sometimes events leave you feeling powerless. In addition to natural disasters, there are political upheavals, business downturns and aggressive competitors who seem to appear out of nowhere. We cannot control the world around us, although we generally can affect our small sphere of influence. Can we make a difference within the world given those limitations? Of course we can. Being mentally well balanced means that we know and accept that there are limits to our ability to control circumstances.

Only with this self-knowledge can we respond most effectively to situations that are disastrous to our business, at least in the moment.

## Accept What's Inevitable

We all saw the terrible images of people running from the collapsing Twin Towers. Dramatic, world-changing events happen all too frequently. An unpredicted and unprecedented earthquake killed and uprooted hundreds of thousands of people in China. In recent years, we experienced Hurricane Katrina and the tsunami in Southeast Asia. Lightning strikes, and we have to deal with the results.

Mike and Peggy Sarak owned and operated Dejean Milo, the popular $8 million annual revenues, bistro in New Orleans, 10 blocks east of the French Quarter. One Sunday morning in late August, amid predictions of a possible Category 5 hurricane, Mike expected a delivery from Chile. The ship, already heading up the Gulf of Mexico in advance of the storm, had made a stop in Houston. Its next and final stop was New Orleans. Peggy agreed to take the children to her sister's home in Baton Rouge, and Mike agreed to meet her there before the storm hit land. Unfortunately, things spun out of control. The ship from Houston was late coming in. The refrigeration system at the restaurant shorted out and Mike's electrician had left town the day before to avoid the storm.

At nightfall, Mike returned to his home in the Garden District to pick up his luggage. He remembers sitting on the couch, exhausted, for a brief respite before making the two-hour drive to safety. In his next moment of wakeful consciousness after his unplanned nap, Mike heard the howling wind and then the lights went out. Within a half hour, he was stranded in his home. Mike did eventually find his way to Baton Rouge—two days later. When he and Peggy returned to New Orleans after a few weeks, Dejean Milo was a puddle of soaked lumber.

I relate this sad tale because misfortune happens every day to people like you and me. In retrospect, it's easy to fault Mike for not leaving New Orleans earlier. However, as a responsible businessperson, he made a judgment call to wait for the delivery from Chile and to fix his refrigeration system once it shorted out in order to protect his inventory from spoiling. Neither Mike nor anyone else knew then that Katrina would have the far-reaching effects that it did.

## React for Survival

Three years after Hurricane Katrina, I visited Mike and Peggy at their newly renovated restaurant. They revealed the tools they used to survive the loss of $8 million in revenues and the emotional trauma they suffered as a result of the destruction of Dejean Milo. Mike said, "I could have thrown it all away. At first I blamed myself. Then, I started to view this calamity as a wake-up call. I stopped saying 'disaster' when I realized we were too caught up in the drama and it wasn't healthy. I started to use the word 'opportunity,' for lack of a better word. The reality was there was nothing else I could do. I stopped complaining and wishing it didn't happen."

Peggy talked about the difficulty of feeling powerless while wanting to do something. Many of their employees never returned to New Orleans. Suppliers canceled contracts. Insurance companies were not forthcoming with commitments to pay for damage or replacement. It was unclear if federal relief would be sufficient. Peggy knew it was not good to make changes only to alleviate anxiety. With so many unknowns, it was important to wait.

When I told them I was in awe of their courage, Peggy assured me that what appeared courageous was a daily and sometimes hourly decision. In retrospect, coping appears much easier.

## Mobilize Quickly

Both Peggy and Mike spoke about how the urgency of the situation mobilized people. Mike recalled, "The employees that remained were the heroes of Dejean Milo. They came through. A few people took leadership roles, cheering others on, assigning tasks, conveying a wonderful future. This was amazing, since these leaders suffered, too. One young man lost everything he owned. His mother was found dead in her home. Yet he kept going. His compassion for all of us was a miracle. Though he had no psychological training, he encouraged us to meet at the end of each day and discuss our reactions. My faith in human nature peaked during that time."

Mike continued, "After a couple of weeks, the company took on a life of its own. Peggy and I initially went along for the ride. Morale began to skyrocket and changes took place—real changes." He added, with a bit of wonder in his voice, "In fact, the company is better now than it ever was."

Mike and Peggy's story highlights three key takeaways for *responding to disaster*. First, they framed the disaster as a wake-up call and were explicit about avoiding drama as they dealt with the situation. Next, Peggy mentioned not doing "something" only to alleviate anxiety. Third, they spoke about how a small group of leaders emerged and mobilized the company to move forward.

### Communicate Broadly

In all cases when people in business mobilize around the urgency to move forward, excitement and momentum are generated by communicating successes. We all need reminders of our courage and our achievements as we move forward in life. It is far too easy to forget our heroism and go back to business as usual. Communicating successes broadly, both inside and outside the company, is cited as the single most important factor by every business affected by disasters. This maintains forward momentum and sustainable business growth.

Disasters notwithstanding, we *can* create a PROFITS culture with a sense of commitment and clearly articulated goals. Perhaps the essential lesson we learn from disasters is that people do have the courage to band together and mobilize to action. How can we make this happen in our daily work?

## COMMITTING TO YOUR BUSINESS

Being committed to your business means doing whatever it takes to achieve your definition of success. Entrepreneurs know what they want and they *go for it*. You know it is arduous to stick to a plan because entrepreneurs are not typically the most patient or detail-oriented individuals.

- *Agree on your overall direction*
- *Craft aggressive and realistic goals*

You may set goals only to decide on a different goal when another idea comes to mind. The rigor of following a plan is difficult, even though you may find it easy to write a new one. As new ideas hatch and old ones go by the wayside, you may find yourself with some of this and some of that. The resulting lack of focus can quickly drain your energy. Commitment and follow-through keep you on course when things get difficult.

You may find the following steps beneficial for mobilizing your company to action, to create consensus about what is important, and to accomplish the results you want.

## Agree on Your Overall Direction

Sometimes prioritizing your current direction is painful for companies when your management team or board of directors are not in agreement. Endless disputes about agenda top the list of difficulties faced by many small and medium-sized business owners. As a result, their companies hobble along, changing direction in reaction to every customer request. Frequently labeled creative, but actually highly destructive, chaos is the consequence of a company that operates without a road map. What essential factors must we address to increase profitability of our business?

- What is urgent?
- What is long-term?
- What is short-term?
- What is realistic?
- What is visionary?

As the head of a profitable company, you probably have many irons in the fire. Sometimes you may be solving a specific problem like increasing market share for a losing product line. At another time, you may think about starting a consultative function to aid customers in finding creative solutions to their problems. Although dealing with such issues is vital, your commitment to your overall direction and goals is what keeps you fired up.

Perhaps you can benefit from the approach taken in the next example. Skylar Paper Goods, in western New York, is a $6 million company offering full-service office support. The partners struggled with their direction. John Netburn and Bob Rogers launched Skylar in 1981 by selling paper for Xerox copiers. Ten years later, John realized that his customers' customers, the end users of their product, worked in large corporate office parks across western New York and needed a variety of services associated with the paper they bought. Bob disagreed at first. However, as they talked about their vision for the future and actions for success, it became apparent to both John and Bob that Skylar could reap greater profits by offering new services to its corporate clients, including typing, report formatting, designing slide presentations and full-service packages at premium prices. Skylar was able to offer 12-hour turnaround time for all work orders started by 4:00 PM daily by employing 20 freelance consultants across western New York and Pennsylvania covering an 18-hour workday. Profits increased by 400 percent in the first year.

## Craft Aggressive and Realistic Goals

Resolving conflicting beliefs about a company's overall direction is not easy, but clarifying priorities will aid in the process of crafting aggressive and realistic goals. One insightful method for agreement on goals is to clarify core capabilities. Building and leveraging your strengths and choosing only a few goals helps you focus. By doing so, you validate the value you add for your customer.

Once you verify your core capabilities, you set goals that are simpler to achieve. For example, Terra Plantworks, a $3 million retailer of floral arrangements, selling regionally in the mid-Atlantic states, had flat revenues for three consecutive quarters. When she took a hard look at her business, CEO Phyllis Strong discovered that the company's core capabilities were merchandising and distribution. Although they planted seeds that grew into flowers, this part of the business was costly and burdensome to Phyllis and her partner. Eventually, they decided to purchase high-quality mature plants directly from growers and focus more of their time strengthening distribution, merchandising, and marketing, as well as developing a consultation practice for florists. They sold most of their greenhouses and built a small showroom. Three years after changing their model, Terra Plantworks is a focused, integrated company with $11 million in annual revenue. With 85 percent of customer purchases resulting from online sales, including 1–800-Flowers, profit margins have grown to a whopping 46 percent. Phyllis Strong carefully reviewed her organization's ability to achieve realistic goals.

Think about your company's goals. Before moving forward, answer the following questions:

- Does your organization have the ability to achieve its goals?
- Do your people have the skills and knowledge to complete these goals based on agreed-upon time lines? If not, are you changing your goals and/or training your people in response?
- Are goals aggressive, challenging, and still doable?
- What goals can you achieve right now?
- Are you choosing the right goals? Too many? Too few?

Since crafting aggressive goals is so important, here is another example for you to consider.

Tira Boutique is a chain of 10 boutiques across the country, headquartered in Greenwich, Connecticut, with annual revenues of $32 million. Tira's goal was to upgrade sales associate's skills and increase profit margins to offset the increasing costs for operating the boutiques in high-rent neighborhoods.

Until three years ago, the owners of Tira hired the sales force based on their likable personalities and many employees did not have previous selling experience. An aspect of Tira's employee retention strategy was to pay salespeople top dollar based on the competition of other boutiques on chic Greenwich Avenue.

Then, the manager in the San Diego office suggested implementing a weekly conference call for all store managers, buyers, planners, and merchandisers. During these calls, the salespeople shared their best and worst-selling merchandise of the week, even though there were significant regional differences among the stores. They also discussed ideas for increasing store traffic, dealing with competition, and reducing expenses. The most exciting discussions centered on successful sales practices. The next year, Tira Boutique established a partnership with a high-end cosmetics company to increase profit margins.

As a result of the conference calls, stores carried a more varied mix of merchandise and salespeople utilized exciting strategies for cross-selling and obtaining repeat business. The partnership with the cosmetics company increased profit margins by 12 percent in the first year while increasing sales by 30 percent.

Venator Group, known to many for its flagship Foot Locker brand, skirted bankruptcy by taking the time to identify its core capabilities. With a strong new merchandising team, management decided to focus on the Foot Locker brand and close 467 Kinney Shoes stores, taking a $173 million charge. Afterthoughts, Venator's jewelry accessory chain, was sold to Claires for $250 million. In 2007, Foot Locker's total sales dipped to $5.4 billion from $5.75 billion in 2006, although the company still tops the industry. Profit margins also fell, largely due to store closings and related costs. Though this seems like a negative statistic, the actions taken to close the stores were a long-term strategy to stay in business.

Thorough knowledge of your core capabilities leads to aggressive and realistic goals. When these goals are transparent at every level of the company, you ensure coordinated energy, concentration, and commitment.

As you will see next, goals and commitments exist within a world of uncertainty. How then is it possible to make decisions under these conditions?

## DEALING WITH UNCERTAINTY

Dealing with uncertainty is a given in the business world and differs from the earlier discussion about disasters. How can you truly commit to your business direction when it is virtually impossible for your company to be synchronized with market changes? A company's design would be able to change as quickly as the environment for that to be the case. There is even greater complexity in this equation because aspects of the market change at different rates—some incrementally and some radically. In addition, random events can occur at any time. Yet, you still need to commit to your goals, formulate your strategic direction, and keep your sanity.

Our major tasks as business owners are to manage around uncertainty and commit to our goals. As we learn to manage risk better, we can work within the current market environment and plan contingencies for changes. Consider how the following actions benefit your ability to deal with uncertainty:

- *Know your risks*
- *Check your assumptions*
- *Act now and do something*

Dealing with uncertainty is the single most defining capability that distinguishes you as a successful entrepreneur, whether you own your own company or run a business unit within a large corporation (intrapreneur). Making decisions becomes more complex when you have greater responsibility and accountability. Many times the outcomes of your decisions are ambiguous and without guarantees. What sets you apart as an entrepreneur is your confidence, judgment, and continued commitment to your business, while carefully managing your risks. The following are some guidelines to help you deal with the uncertainty of your decisions.

## Know Your Risks

Entrepreneurs are risk takers. Risk is never comfortable, although some risk takers may find it exhilarating. Unlike the gambler in Las Vegas or at the racetrack, you can learn to assess your risks. These may be external and include things like regulatory processes, industry-specific factors, taxation changes, government interventions such as price controls, energy and utilities changes, and environmental issues such as pollution controls, zoning, and wildlife laws.

Industry-specific risks may include demand characteristics, customer requirements, supplier considerations, asset risk, asset utilization (driven by demand), finance availability, and other factors pertaining to your particular industry. Usually, risk includes all of these, as well as financial risks of numerous persuasions.

The smart entrepreneur views risk as a key element of the company strategy. How do you perceive risk and operate day to day within your uncertain market environment? One way is to check your assumptions and correct those that may prevent you from viewing uncertainty realistically.

## Check Your Assumptions

Our beliefs have an effect on all that we do. And what we do now affects the future. Having incorrect beliefs can be particularly dangerous in business, where groupthink assumptions result in common group mind-sets. Once groupthink sets in, people are less likely to question assumptions they share. If these assumptions underlie strategic actions, particularly if market conditions change, your business can ultimately be in jeopardy. Some common assumptions are:

- Our larger market share is more important than our profit margins.

**71**

- Our high quality is more important to the customer than speed and lower pricing.
- Our brand will always attract premium prices.
- Streamlining our business and cost containment will keep us competitive.

When you are the business leader, your assumptions influence everyone else in your company for better or worse.

## Act Now and Do Something

Taking action can alleviate an overwhelming sense of uncertainty. Here are some things you can do to get moving in constructive ways with minimal risk. All of them will help you avoid the paralysis that accompanies making decisions within uncertain circumstances.

- Start taking small and calculated risks by trying something new even when you are not sure of the results. For example, add a new measurement to one of your goals.
- Visualize a situation and rehearse three possible outcomes—one that is successful, one that is neutral, and one that is a failure. Notice your reactions to each scenario and imagine what your next step would be.
- Role-play various worst-case scenarios and imagine yourself explaining them to people within your company. Be sure to devise contingency plans in advance.
- Allow yourself to have "incompletions." Prepare *only part* of a presentation. Either ask someone else to complete it or go to a meeting without the entire presentation finished.
- Teach a course that includes subject matter you are not entirely well-versed in. Admit this to your audience.

You can learn to deal successfully with uncertainty. The more you practice, the better you will be and the easier this becomes. The more congruent your beliefs and assumptions are with reality and its uncertainties, the better the prognosis is for running a profitable and successful company. This implies that we let go of people, things, and circumstances that no longer work for our company or ourselves.

## LETTING GO

As we get comfortable with the notion of uncertainty, we can learn when to let go of the unnecessary, trusting we will deal with the consequences productively. Taking the actions to let go include:

- *Build your core*
- *Outsource inefficiencies*
- *Move on*

How do we know when it is time to let go? This is difficult whenever we commit strongly to a financial and emotional course of action. We do not want to accept that things are not working as planned. We want to give it one last shot ... and another and another.

### Build Your Core

You've assessed your internal systems and know your company's strengths. You're focusing on the greatest value for your customers and employing resources that build your unique attributes. You're doing all the right things to ensure your competitive advantage. You also know that no company is good at everything. To deal with their limitations, Fortune 100 companies may partner with companies that have strong capabilities in areas that are not their own core capabilities. They purchase these capabilities from other companies.

### Outsource Inefficiencies

In the past, to outsource was to admit failure. Now, the ability to identify areas for outsourcing is a competitive advantage that allows you to remain focused on your strengths. The next example is an illustration of a company that considered outsourcing as a solution for two different revenue opportunities.

Obary, Inc. is a $4 billion conglomerate whose $200 million Pennsylvania-based ChildPlay division had experienced 10 years of flat annual revenues, which varied by only about 1 percent up or down every year. The parent company maintained three ChildPlay plants—one in the United States, one in China, and one in South Korea. ChildPlay product lines included a Slinky-like knockoff, a variety of toy cars and a line of hanging ceiling mobiles, all made of a coil steel alloy that Obary's industrial materials unit produced. ChildPlay enjoyed high market share in North America and Europe in 2007, but due to commoditization of steel alloy, Obary executives were forecasting lower sales and return on investment for the next few years.

It was time for Obary to face reality. One approach was to sell ChildPlay for cash to a Chinese competitor. With the cash from the sale, Obary would develop an energy-saving device for the water sprinkling systems manufactured at its $25 million, Idaho-based SprinkleTime division. Although SprinkleTime expected to earn high margins on the energy-saving device, this was a new business that would require an investment in training to educate the sales force about the operations, technology, and customer base.

Another approach was to outsource manufacturing of the energy-saving device to an Israeli competitor. This could be more profitable since the Israeli company had strong capabilities in energy-saving devices, where Obary was weak. As it faced reality, Obary chose to outsource to its competitor, which was initially dismissed as a distasteful option.

In the meantime, Obary, Inc. continued to hold on to ChildPlay, adding a few new products and streamlining operations. ChildPlay sales climbed 4 percent two years later and grew 7 percent the following year, when overall industry sales stayed flat. Obary had wisely remained in the toy segment it knew well. In mid-2008, an overseas company with supply chain capability within the toy industry approached Obary for an outsourcing opportunity with ChildPlay. This overseas company had access to inexpensive resources, new markets, and more advanced logistics than ChildPlay. This alliance worked well for ChildPlay. With the increased profits, ChildPlay upgraded its research and development division for innovation of new products.

The key takeaways from this case are to stay within your company's areas of capability and to seize strategic opportunities to outsource inefficiencies.

## Move On

There are times when we need to move on. Interesting projects that we have fully evaluated for risk and potential profits call to us. Customer demand for new and different products, sometimes based on competitor introductions and differentiation, force our hand. To stay in business we must go with the tide. Our continuing practice of crafting aggressive, realistic goals in a world of uncertainty teaches us to let go and move on when necessary, even when we are not fully ready.

The best way to realistically know when to move on is to obtain vital information and then to utilize this information to our company's advantage. Information provides the knowledge for decision making. *Obtain Vital Information* is the PROFITS principle you will read about next.

## SUMMARY

*Reality* underscores the importance of separating fact from fantasy and differentiating what we can and cannot control. You read about Jonas CD/DVD and the company's struggle with a changing market. Management contemplated critical decisions concerning the future of the company. First, the management team recognized the facts of the financial situation. They cut through the complexity and focused intensely on satisfying their customers by becoming a formidable competitor.

Later, we considered the lack of control we possess in disaster situations. We learned to respond successfully to losses, as in the case of Mike and Peggy Sarak, by accepting what is inevitable, reacting appropriately for survival, mobilizing our staff quickly, and broadly communicating successes. What *we can control* is our commitment to our business.

We can accomplish winning results when management agrees on an overall direction and then crafts aggressive and realistic goals based on this direction. We commit to our business, as in life, within a context of uncertainty and learn to minimize risks. Within an uncertain market, we can anticipate many of the risks, check our assumptions about our business and the marketplace, and then take action.

One of the most difficult situations entrepreneurs deal with is letting go of business initiatives that we committed to that are no longer working. Though initially painful, by building our core, outsourcing inefficiencies, and moving on to new projects, we can let go and energize ourselves for an exciting future.

## QUESTIONS AND ACTIONS FOR YOUR BUSINESS PROFITS

- How does your company's current financial performance match projections?
  - → Pinpoint at least one discrepancy (i.e., inventory turnover) and trace all the relationships this has to every other financial and operational practice. Where possible, determine the cost of this discrepancy over one year.
- What are the top three commitments to your business?
  - → Articulate these commitments at every meeting or presentation you attend.
  - → Keep a daily journal for three months and document what you do to address these commitments every day.
- Do you identify and manage discrepancies between your customers' perceptions and your perceptions of your company?

- → Obtain customer feedback regarding their expectations of your operations, return/warranty policies, products, and marketing.
- → Make a commitment to fix any gaps that are revealed.
- What are your three primary strategies to deal with uncertainty?
  - → Create a cross-functional team to design a project that up until now involved too many uncertainties to tackle.
- What project or initiative is struggling and draining resources?
  - → Review your commitment to this project and then determine if you can let it go.
  - → Take steps to radically move the project forward quickly or terminate it within the next two months.

| P | Position Only for Growth |
| R | Reality |
| O | Obtain Vital Information |
| F | Flexibility |
| I | Integration |
| T | Test and Revise |
| S | Steering the Company |

**CHAPTER 5**

# Obtain Vital Information

*To keep a lamp burning, we have to keep oil in it.*

—Mother Teresa

**A**n essential ingredient of a thriving business is discovering *vital information*. How do you make sure you're focused on knowing all that's important and excluding the rest? You're probably doing a lot of the right things already. Do you practice these?

- *Decide what you're looking for*
- *Rely primarily on customer information*
- *Network in and out*
- *Communicate your focus*

Tony, CEO of a $600 million private asset fund, recalls a high school history assignment: "I would wake up on a cold Saturday morning in January during my high school years in Burlington, Vermont, knowing it would take most of the day to research my term paper. I'd trudge to the town library and spend at least an hour at the card catalog, trying to find enough information for my topic. I might find a book or two and a couple of journal articles if I was lucky. Now, my 13-year-old son wakes up to his iPod, strolls to his desk, turns on the computer, opens up his browser and surfs Google for information, downloads and prints it in seconds as he instant messages a few friends, plays a video game, and edits his Facebook data. Most mind-boggling, he does this all at the same time. When he emerges from his room three hours later, cell phone in hand, my son informs me that he changed his original topic based on input from friends in his various online networks. And the person he communicated with that morning who influenced his topic most lives in Tibet."

One of my clients, Jhomar, owns a medium-sized sportswear business catering to well-to-do urban professionals. In a conversation a few days ago, Jhomar, overwhelmed with the amount of industry data he had to read daily, told me about his exasperating day:

"I've discovered LinkedIn," he began. "I simply filled out a profile after a colleague invited me to join his network. I then checked off the names of some of my contacts in my Yahoo! address book and clicked on the small 'invite' icon. Within 20 minutes, I had 65 e-mails from people I hadn't heard from in at least a year. As I clicked on their LinkedIn pages and viewed their profiles, my elation turned to excitement as I saw what seemed like infinite possibilities for new business connections, both in my industry and in related ones. I wanted to stop everything else I was doing and focus on networking."

He continued, "Then I recalled the delivery I'd promised a large wholesaler to be sent out by 5:00 PM and the supplier I'd promised to contact about a new product line. Also, my inventory management retail database and product cost analysis data arrived today. Additionally, I have access to real-time details about every aspect of my business. I know I should stay focused, yet I find myself going off on all sorts of interesting tangents. These aren't a waste of time, because in the long run the information is good and I can squirrel it away for later, but it all just takes so much time."

After another 15 minutes, Jhomar, exhausted from his soliloquy, asked what he might do differently. As he realized, though information is beneficial and advantageous for your business, it can also be seductive and distracting. Focusing your quest for information helps you make the most of your research time.

## DECIDE WHAT YOU'RE LOOKING FOR

How can we make sense of all the data available to us? And how often do we sidestep what we are looking for and start along a new path, ending up more confounded than before? We seduce and distract ourselves on the Internet by following links that are only marginally related to what we need. We rationalize that these voyages will offer a greater understanding of our subject. This may be true, yet another hour or more slips away on an unplanned adventure. Usually other work, dinner or sleep is the casualty of these indulgences.

As you consider your purpose for exploring data and *vital information*, let's differentiate between them. *Data* (datum in plural) refers to facts. When you process, organize, and structure data it can become useful information. Information is transformed data that businesses exploit to find patterns, trends, and other ways to supplement knowledge they may have. With this in mind, the first steps to finding the *vital information* you need are to:

- *Clarify your purpose*
- *Search data to your purpose*
- *Avoid analysis paralysis*

Reflecting on a question, problem, or opportunity for your business provides the focus to organize your thoughts and find what you need.

## Clarify Your Purpose

The babble of extraneous data can distract you for days. When you clarify your purpose for seeking data, you reinforce what is important for your business. You can begin by asking the following questions:

- What problem or opportunity requires a solution?
- What information is currently missing?
- What are my knowledge gaps on X?
- How will additional data help me solve this?

At this point, you may want to review the three key questions posed previously (Chapter 2, *PROFITS*; Chapter 3, *Position Only for Growth*).

1. *What do I want to accomplish?*
2. *What is the current state of my business?*
3. *What is required for my company to become more profitable?*

These questions help to focus your pursuit of data. The answers will reinforce your commitment to your strategic direction or suggest alternative positioning for your business. With this clarity, you can search more effectively for information to help serve your customers and clarify the core capabilities you need for the future of your business.

For example, your business may currently choose speed over low cost or margin over market share. You may position your company for innovation, as employer of choice, for service leadership, for operational efficiency, or as an outsourcing partner, to name a few possibilities. With so much competition globally, most companies need three or more core capabilities to win the race. As you fine-tune your purpose, find the most current and reliable information you can to develop or outsource the core capabilities your business requires. *Most information you seek should be for the purpose of enriching and fortifying a strategic direction that serves your customers and positions your company for future profitability.*

There is always new information available about business. Certainly, you want to learn as much as you can about your customers and the end users of your products or services (your customers' customers). When researching your customers, ask yourself questions that deepen your understanding of your mission and what your competitors might offer that you don't:

- Why is this company a competitor?
- What are the similarities among its customers (e.g., industry, product line, its customers' customers)?
- What competitive advantages does the company have when compared to its competitors other than my business (e.g., pricing, speed to market, customer service)?
- What do I want to know about my competitor's operations, sales strategy, and long-term goals?

## Search Data to Your Purpose

How do you sift all the available information to find only what you need to help you make sound decisions? It is worthwhile to know the best sources of information for your business. Many industries have web sites, research reports, or other sources that already mined through the more mainstream data. They have experts who take this data and transform it into trends and patterns. In fact, once transformed, this data is sometimes called intelligence. Though costly, these sources can save hours of time. They are particularly beneficial if your company does not have a research department or if transforming data is not one of your core capabilities.

Sometimes data you find may not appear to fit, based on your experience and knowledge of the customer and industry. Rather than discount the data, especially if it comes from a reliable source, identify and explore these anomalies. Doing so can help you hone your expertise and learn to convert the information you uncover into useful opportunities. Working with anomalies will improve your questioning skills, sometimes can redefine the specifics of your search, and can sharpen your critical thinking.

A discussion of searching data would be incomplete without discussing the phenomenon called multitasking. With all we have to accomplish, most of us continuously search for and accumulate data for more than one task at a time. The following example illustrates this point.

Mary Ellen, COO of a $20 million consumer products company, has three deadlines this week. There is little commonality between her tasks. Additionally, Mary Ellen participates in several conference calls each day. Handling more than 100 e-mails daily and ongoing interruptions throughout the workday, Mary Ellen believes she is an excellent multitasker.

Though we all multitask to some degree, UCLA and University of Michigan researchers recently discovered that the time and effort utilized in switching back and forth between tasks results in less concentrated attention to details, poor information retention, and less productive brain activity. The average workday is usually bursting with interruptions. Most entrepreneurs know how difficult it is to stop the daily noise, so I won't belabor the point. We know that when we need to concentrate or meet an important deadline, we work in the early morning hours, late into the night, or on weekends. Cognitive overload prevents us from processing the overwhelming quantity of data we hold in working memory and from obtaining the necessary rest our brain requires. We are literally clogged with information.

## Avoid Analysis Paralysis

Almost everyone uses the Internet, cell phones and personal digital assistants (PDAs), blogs, podcasts, chat rooms, journals and books, and we are all on information overload. How can we find only the *vital information* we need to focus on and avoid the immobility that sometimes results from having too much data?

To avoid immobility, sometimes called analysis paralysis, ask yourself the following questions: Will the information help me take action and enable better decisions? When does the risk of an unprofitable decision outweigh the cost of further research? The more clarity you have about what you are seeking, the lower the likelihood of paralysis.

We will never have all the information we need and there are no guarantees for success. At some point, we must draw the proverbial line in the sand and take action, relying on both facts and intuition. We then allow additional filtered information to help us correct course for the duration of our projects. Your ability to focus on a purpose and then search for the vital information directs you to know when you have 'good enough' information to avoid paralysis and move your business forward.

Confirm your assumptions before you begin your research. Ask people with differing perspectives for feedback and then take action. Unpredictability and the onslaught of continuous data have many implications for how you manage your customers, who suffer from their own data overload. Your ability to help your customers manage their uncertainty and avoid analysis paralysis can be one of your competitive advantages, leading directly to stronger profitability for you and for them.

The information you obtain from your customers is what's most important for your company's success. You may supplement this information with other sources, but let this be the information that structures your goals.

## RELY PRIMARILY ON CUSTOMER INFORMATION

It is more difficult to keep a customer satisfied today than it was five years ago. Simply meeting customer needs is no longer sufficient. Successful companies anticipate customer wants. Think about the emphasis on customized features for thousands of items you commonly use. Customers can now build and then buy Nike footwear based on choices on Nike's web site. Both BustedTees and Springleap manufacture and sell T-shirts that customers create. We go to a Build-A-Bear Workshop to design stuffed animals for our loved ones. In fact, many companies actually sponsor customer idea and design contests. The winner's creation then becomes the next great product.

Consumers now *expect* choices. Greater supply chain efficiency and cutting-edge technology allow and encourage just-in-time manufacturing and replenishment with less inventory and storage fees. Successful companies have the flexibility to create exactly what customers desire.

Here are some ways for you to acquire the best information about your customers' needs and wants:

- *Live with your customers before you sell*
- *Find valuable customer intelligence*
- *Create cross-functional teams*
- *Educate your customers*

Imagine you are at a party. You lock eyes with a stranger across the room. This is someone you want to get to know. The person approaches with a wide smile. You spend the rest of the evening engaged in stimulating conversation. A warm rapport develops and you increasingly believe you are having a date with destiny. And the question is: Would you marry this person based on one, two, or even three meetings? Most of us, not being clairvoyant, would probably decline a marriage proposal at this point. It is not so different with customers and suppliers.

## Live With Your Customer Before You Sell

How many times has this happened to you? Someone refers a client, and you schedule a meeting. The subsequent conversation ends with the potential client almost promising the sale. He says, "It's just a formality for my boss to sign off on it," but in the end the boss does not sign off. There is a vague promise about getting it finalized "in a few months."

John, a successful management consultant with an organization of 26 employees, spoke about his first year in business. "During the first year, I had at least 20 'almost' contracts. Nearly all my referrals and cold calls appeared successful and although

I concluded most meetings with confidence, I could not get my clients to commit."

"One day," he continued, "after another devastating disappointment, I felt I had been hit over the head with a two-by-four. I realized that in meetings with potential clients, I unknowingly offered my responsibility for closing the deal to someone I had conversed with for little over an hour. How could this person fully explain and educate someone else in their organization about a business that took me years to define? Now I take the time to learn about a prospective client's business, just like I did when I worked for a large Fortune 500 consumer goods company. I ask about the prospect's customers. I meet with the prospect's colleagues in a variety of functional areas and bring some of my people with similar expertise to the table. Although we share our knowledge and educate the prospective client about our company, rarely do we anticipate or focus attention on the sale. And we also remain in close contact with customers at times when our company is not involved in projects with them. This ongoing involvement fortifies the relationship and brings awareness of potential hot spots for the customer that we revisit at a more opportune time."

John continued, "As a result of this approach to our business, by the time we sign a contract, my company has already demonstrated reliability, dependability, and commitment. We've gained a significant amount of client proprietary information because of the trust built during this courtship phase. Our success is now stellar, and I'm proud to say we rarely lose a client."

### Find Valuable Customer Intelligence

Successful business owners often complain about a sales cycle that seems to be too lengthy. Others, like John, welcome this courtship, using the time to supplement vital and valuable customer intelligence. This is how business units sometimes operate in a Fortune 100 company. John finds out what his customers truly aspire to. Do they want to be green, child-friendly, morally good? Do they want a partner that is global, local, urban-friendly, wealthy, friendly? Is this customer's mission congruent with their business model and image? John's greatest value to his customers is helping them integrate their mission and business model with those of their own customers. He helps his customers maintain an outward focus and teaches them to find creative solutions for helping their own customers succeed. Finding and providing valuable customer intelligence is a winning proposition for John, his customers and his customers' customers—something that can easily be passed forward even further.

Since this is such an essential topic, here is another example.

Paul Oster designs blown-glass vases in Charleston, South Carolina and enjoyed revenues in 2008 of $25 million. Although Paul rents space in an upscale furniture showroom, most of the time he operates B to Z at his home office.

When not designing, Paul surfs the Internet, following global design trends to find valuable customer intelligence that he shares with customers, potential customers and suppliers. He tracks other glass and pottery artists, accessing sales statistics from museums, trade shows, retail stores and boutiques around the world. Along with input triggered by his own web site, his blog, and his membership in several online user groups and communities, Paul quickly learns about his competition and adapts his business as trends and consumer demands shift.

An international supply chain company recruits the B to Z global and local sales force in 50 countries. It also distributes and delivers merchandise to B to Z customers within 24 hours of every customer purchase. Each sale generates an alert to replenish the item for future sales and distribution. This same supply chain company provides the option for financing B to Z materials and handling receivables and payables. Customer orders route to a busy call center in India. Paul receives questions from India in real time on his Palm Treo from call center representatives, customers, or the sales force.

Trend watchers and customers provide rave reviews on Internet feedback sites, writing about Paul's ability to spot best-value trends for his customers and about his outstanding knowledge of the industry. Paul created a winning prototype for both his business and his customers—and few people know that he functions like a Fortune 100 company in the comfort of his South Carolina beach house.

The key takeaway from B to Z is that you, like Paul Oster, can use a combination of ingenuity and data sources to create the profitable business you always dreamed of.

## Create Cross-Functional Teams

Paul devised a complex net of teams within his business. Since most smaller businesses do not have the resources to develop every function in-house, many companies find cross-functional and intercompany teams valuable.

Creating cross-functional teams that include various functions within your company and your customer's company has many advantages for *obtaining vital information*. Intercompany cooperation (between different companies) contributes a wide array of talent and expertise because of the varied perspectives of the people involved. This builds stronger relationships and trust. Both you and your customers can obtain feedback and vital information to fine-tune assumptions and uncover additional customer needs and desires. When experts within various functions such as marketing, research and development, finance, and operations participate on these teams, you acquire a broader portrait of your customer. You have opportunities to educate each other by providing specialized knowledge. If your company is small and you do not have several distinctive functional areas, you can partner with other companies and invite them to be on the team. This is not cheating, only good business sense. Paul, in the example, very successfully shaped both cross-functional and cross-company teams.

## Educate Your Customers

In addition to the products or services you offer them, always think of yourself as an information provider for your customers. Whether you speak to your customers in person or offer information on the Internet, you can educate your customers by supplying vital information and increasing their ability to be profitable and valuable to their own customers. Information can pertain to predicting new trends in your customers' customers' key markets, locating vital information about future innovations, identifying global supply chain efficiencies, and differentiating competitor strengths and weaknesses, to name a few. The best way to acquire and disseminate vital information and expertise is by networking.

## NETWORK IN AND OUT

Of course, networks are valuable in many ways. The purpose here is to discuss how networks are important sources of essential data. More than ever before, successful people rely on other successful people to find the vital information they need to run their businesses. No single person can possibly absorb and quickly find all the information required in a timely manner. It is not only who you know, but who you know who is reliable, responsive, and savvy enough to provide the resources you need when you need them. Viewed from this perspective, networks become your personal business yellow pages. In thinking about networks, keep the following points in mind:

- *Know what you don't know*
- *Create internal alliances*
- *Create external alliances*

### Know What You Don't Know

Most of us build our knowledge base throughout our careers. Many people take in information as a personal learning strategy. Yet the best approach to obtaining information is through an exchange of resources with trusted advisers and colleagues. Those who are politically savvy—and I mean this as a compliment—let others know they are available for sharing their knowledge.

Usually the most relevant vital information comes from other members of our own project teams with talents that differ from our own.

Florence, an expert in global steel markets and an associate professor of metallurgy in Belgium, speaks and writes frequently on this topic. She is a member of a small entrepreneurs group that frequently attends a variety of global conferences and consultations. Florence compensates for what she sees as her lack of expertise in other markets by co-authoring many of her articles with local experts who can provide information to audiences about alternative building materials. She and her coterie of fellow entrepreneurs also serve as referral sources for each other and frequently work on the same projects.

As result, Florence and her colleagues extend their areas of expertise and contribute important global knowledge that would not be possible without their combined efforts.

Like Florence and her colleagues, we can expand our own capabilities, businesses, and profits when we exchange relevant vital information with people on our own project teams with our varied talents.

## Create Internal Alliances

François, the CEO of La Valore Cosmetics, a $65 million company in Paris, France, is building a strong relationship with a U.S. film production company in Burbank, California. François's contact person is the CEO, but he views the entire company as his customer. Based on this perspective, François created a team of five people in his company to accompany him to appointments and meet with various other staff members at the customer company. The CEO of the client company appreciated this approach and believed it would benefit his business.

After their visit, François's team debriefed with their internal networks within La Valore Cosmetics to gain a more inclusive perspective for the team's approach. For example, a question surfaced at the meeting that required additional marketing and technological knowledge. Ralph, La Valore Cosmetics' CIO, offered a comprehensive integrated network solution for the team. Other colleagues shared their personal contacts who had familiarity with the production industry or had firsthand experience with this particular production company.

As a result, François' team, fortified with valuable supplementary information, participated at the next customer meeting and obtained a sizable extended contract. This comprehensive approach to working with the customer provided La Valore Cosmetics with a competitive advantage. Additionally, because François' team learned general and specific information about production companies, a few months later they made a foray into another production company. It is indeed a small world with people constantly on the move in most industries. It is a good bet that you, too, can find the vital information and key people in your targeted markets with a few well-placed e-mails or phone calls, especially if your networking etiquette is skillful.

## Create External Alliances

Max is Vice President of a $200 million branded product line in a Fortune 100 consumer products company. His most recent assignment was to create an interactive marketing site for his new product line in South and Central America. Max's sparse Internet knowledge, limited to online shopping sites and e-mail, required a quick fix.

As he contemplated his choices, Max reflected most seriously on two options. He could jump right in and possibly get lost in the morass on the Internet as he searched for relevant data and information about interactive marketing. Or, he could work his network by identifying other marketers in non-competing companies and asking colleagues for introductions.

The latter option appealed to Max. He started by clarifying his assignment and jotting down questions to move him toward the vital information he desired. He spent 15 minutes identifying people who might have the information he needed. Max decided he could learn most efficiently by speaking to experts across a variety of fields, including technology, marketing, and product development. He conducted quick preliminary Internet research to answer some of the easier questions on his own and began a quick search of companies to find appealing interactive web sites. Max then reviewed business cards of recent conferences he recently attended, beginning with those where he gave presentations, hoping to establish credibility and connect with people who would recall his expertise.

Within an hour, Max had located 10 possible contacts. He spent another hour learning about these people through search engines until he was ready to contact them by telephone and e-mail. These preliminaries provided Max with information to help him personalize his conversations. When calling people, Max introduced himself graciously, asking if it was a good time to speak and then succinctly stated his request for information. He ended his calls with an assurance to follow up. Max also reinforced relationships by giving as well as getting—by offering his support in the future should any of the contacts need his help.

By the end of the day, Max obtained five telephone appointments and one face-to-face meeting scheduled for the next day. Notice the speed with which this approach took place. Most of Max's contacts were only one or two separation points from the people Max sought. His planning prior to the calls, his networking etiquette, and his ability to articulate his needs with precision resulted in quick and fruitful results.

Max's correct assumption was that people with strong network resources value their contacts and provide access to a few chosen others whom they trust. People who refer you to others also appreciate feedback about the responsiveness of their contacts. Handle your connections with respect and care.

## COMMUNICATE YOUR FOCUS

The ability to articulate your focus with clarity is essential. Successful people know they have the responsibility of helping others and supporting them by operating in the following ways:

- *Organize your information*
- *Align your company*
- *Speak and present continuously*

When Jim accepted a job offer from Baldwin MediaWorks, a $35 million marketing company with both full-time and contracted employees, for the position of Vice President of Human Resources, he asked to read the company's mission and goals. He found some inconsistencies within these documents and scheduled an appointment with Marvin McMillian, the CEO.

## Organize Your Information

Prior to meeting with the CEO, Jim attempted to clarify some of the more obvious contradictions by meeting with Penny, the Vice President of Marketing, who Jim recently met at a few staff meetings. Jim perceived Penny as smart, professional, and credible. He believed Penny would add to the perspective he received from his manager, the Senior Vice President of Human Resources. After asking Penny for her understanding of the company mission and goals, Jim focused his thinking in preparation for his meeting with Marvin, the CEO.

## Align Your Company

At the meeting with Marvin, Jim asked how Marvin's goals related to the company goals. Although initially surprised by the question, Marvin realized two things. The first was that Jim was a critical thinker who would be an asset to the company, and the second was that Marvin's own goals did not align with the mission and goals agreed upon at the annual retreat a few months earlier.

As a result of this short meeting, Marvin, the CEO, asked for a review of all staff goals within the company. Though the review was time-consuming, it was a critical endeavor with far-reaching ramifications for the future success of the company. It was certainly worth the time expended with 125 employees over a six-week time frame. Marvin knew that without consistent, aligned and clearly articulated goals, the company could not focus on the few important priorities.

### Speak and Present Continuously

As part of this review process at Baldwin MediaWorks, the expectation was for each employee to articulate the company message to others within the company to ensure a consistent, clear understanding of the business mission. A presentation skills course, similar to one conducted at a local Fortune 100 company, became an annual requirement for the top 50 people in the business to hone their ability to express information with clarity and confidence since they interfaced frequently with customers and other company stakeholders. A customer satisfaction feedback questionnaire, distributed a few months later, reinforced that the clear company message did provide vital information to define Baldwin MediaWorks.

### SUMMARY

*Vital information* comes from many sources. To find and utilize this information, first clarify your information needs and then execute a focused search for data that avoids analysis paralysis. Remember that the most critical data for your company usually relies on customer information. A good strategy for obtaining this information is to live with your customers before you sell to them, finding hot spots for current and future customer wants and desires. Cross-functional teams can enhance your perspective by providing a variety of viewpoints. Finally, be sure to remember that you are a source of vital information for your customers, and it is important to find opportunities to educate them about the industry, current market trends, and competitor attributes.

Networking is often the most efficient source of vital information. Proficiency at networking means knowing what you do not know and creating internal and external alliances. Network etiquette is essential for strengthening ongoing relationships and acquiring the information you want quickly. Finally, communicate your focus by organizing your information, aligning your company and taking opportunities to present information about your company continuously.

## QUESTIONS AND ACTIONS FOR YOUR BUSINESS PROFITS

- What is your usual approach to finding vital information for a new project?
- Think of a potential customer.
    - → What vital information is important to learn about him or her?
    - → How will you find this vital information?
    - → How will you work with this customer?
- Think about this potential customer or a current customer.
    - → What cross-functional teams will be beneficial for both you and your customer?
    - → What vital information will each team provide in meeting your customer's needs?
- Think about people in your network.
    - → How can you strengthen your relationships?
    - → What can you do to expand your network?
- What do you want people to know about your company?
- What venues can you utilize to articulate your vision?

| P | Position Only for Growth |
|---|---|
| R | Reality |
| O | Obtain Vital Information |
| F | Flexibility |
| I | Integration |
| T | Test and Revise |
| S | Steering the Company |

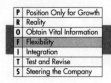

## CHAPTER 6

# Flexibility

*Leaders honor their core values, yet they are flexible in how they execute them.*

—Colin Powell

What does it mean to be *flexible*? How can you develop a culture of *flexibility* in your business? In the current fast-paced and fickle marketplace, companies must respond to customers' changing requirements quickly. For many companies, flexibility means adapting quickly to core targeted customers—a competitive advantage well worth honing.

You can accelerate the implementation of a culture of flexibility by applying these actions:

- *Champion change*
- *Be an influencer*
- *Foster interactive communication*
- *Create processes*
- *Do it now*

The *flexibility* of Jim Burns, CEO of Jonas CD/DVD (Chapter 4, *Reality*), saved the struggling company when he proposed a new business plan to his investors. As you may recall, the company had to reinvent itself immediately or go out of business within six months.

Skeeter Footwear (Chapter 3, *Position Only for Growth*), the company that distributes moderate-priced footwear to boutiques and large upscale retail chains, offers another example of adaptation and flexibility for future survival and prosperity.

After Sean Meyer became Skeeter's CEO in 2000, the company's sales slipped along with the rest of the athletic shoe sector due to bad publicity globally about business practices such as child labor. Sean made what appeared to be a drastic decision to opt out of the premium price point, primarily because of the expense of carrying increasingly overstocked inventory.

Sean's research helped him identify the compelling trend that females between the ages of 8 and 18, a growing demographic, preferred shopping for moderate-price-point footwear in upscale stores. In response, Sean devised a creative and flexible approach for transforming his business model and redesigning Skeeter's internal processes. By targeting both the upscale stores and the young female demographic, Skeeter Footwear increasingly built customer loyalty in the upscale stores by selling a superior product in the midprice range and creating a competitive advantage.

## WHAT FLEXIBILITY IS AND IS NOT

In an entrepreneur management course, the professor asked students for a definition of *flexibility*, and these were some responses: "Flexibility is a creative flow and isn't encumbered by rules." "There is a lack of control and discipline." "Things organize naturally, without effort." "New ideas surface. People build on each other's thoughts and adapt to the current reality." "You have to adapt to what people need. It's not about you." "Creativity has free rein." Some of the definitions seemed almost romantic, even more surprising considering this discussion took place in a business class.

To be effective, there must be some structure when practicing *flexibility*. Yet not one person in the entrepreneur class included the words *processes, discipline, boundaries,* or *planning* in the definition. Unbounded, uncontrolled, and undisciplined flexibility is not flexibility at all. It is chaos. Anyone who works for a company for any length of time can cite many examples of the phenomenon I'll call "flexibility chaos."

From new business start-ups to product development in large companies, chaos can reign across a range of business situations. For some companies, order may organically evolve from experience and the repetition of repeated work procedures. Yet the evolution of order is more complicated, when it involves multiple tasks and functional areas. I worked for a successful Fortune 100 company where people would proclaim, "Look how successful we are. Imagine how profitable we would be if the right hand knew what the left was doing. Our isolated functions do not work together. Finance doesn't consult with marketing about pricing. Operations are set apart from the rest of the company and do not communicate with sales. Salespeople are out in the field making promises to customers without engineering or operations validating the probability of delivering on those promises."

Making it up as you go along, without coordination among the moving parts of the business—what some may call flexibility—is a recipe for disaster.

Then what is effective flexibility? Effective flexibility is responding to new circumstances by designing your business—the structure and processes—to be nimble and to adapt to the speed of change. Flexibility is the ability to respond and adapt continually and to know that change is a fact of life.

## ADAPTING FLEXIBLY TO CHANGE

Say you discover a small company in China that produces your product using comparable materials at half your cost. Would you be able to find comparable suppliers? Do you have distribution mechanisms to support global customers? Questions like these highlight the need for flexible solutions.

Although change is inevitable, some companies respond more quickly than others. Here are several examples:

- *Developing new products.* In the early 1990s, AT&T decreased the time to market for new products from two years to one, before it became fashionable to introduce new phone designs every few months. Sprint, T-Mobile, and Cingular were latecomers to this new model.

- *Customizing products.* General Electric reduced production turnaround from three weeks to three days for custom-made industrial circuits based on specifications that customers demanded. This forced competitors to do the same.

- *Improving existing products on demand.* Japanese firms learned to upgrade products continuously, leaving U.S. companies bewildered—and way behind. The renowned Toyota just-in-time business model changed global businesses by producing better products, reducing inventory and delivering products faster.

- *Delivery of ordered products.* Benetton led the brigade in designing to spec and delivering within one week by using sophisticated handling procedures, streamlining logistics, and adjusting to unexpected trends. Now, other retailers supply limited quantities of their best sellers to create demand for new styles.

- *Adjusting market offers.* Apple offers customers a large array of colors, sizes, and price points for its most popular computers and iPods. Wireless phone companies keep adding new features and quickly rendering their phones, though still usable, obsolete.

- *Answering customer questions.* Banks can approve customer applications in minutes, though this may not be good for the economy in the long run, evidenced by rising housing foreclosures and credit card debt.

An important benefit when your company is ahead of the curve in flexibility is that you suffer less rivalry from competition initially. As an early adopter, you can charge premium prices and use bargaining power and innovation in supplier relationships. By learning from the market, remaining flexible, and adapting continuously, you can maintain your first-mover market position longer. Aside from these benefits, you need to determine if increasing your speed (and stress) works for your company's culture and mission. To instill this flexibility throughout your organization, you need to learn how to champion change.

## CHAMPION CHANGE

Change always requires forethought. Though you may believe a change will not be costly and can be an add-on to what your systems already produce, this is almost never true.

When considering a planned change you need to:

- *Identify expected results*
- *Anticipate market changes*
- *Communicate priorities*
- *Measure effectively*
- *Celebrate success*

Most people initiate change in their businesses because they expect the change to lead to profitable results. Here are some questions to ask yourself when considering a change in your business model. You will come up with others on your own.

- What is the problem or business opportunity this change solves?
- What customer results do you anticipate with the modifications you design and implement for your customers or end users (your customers' customers)?

- Do your customers tend to be early adopters of products and solutions?
- How will the changes affect employees and their ability to provide excellent service?

## Identify Expected Results

Andree Milivan, CEO of Shoppers Square, a $300 million regional building construction/supply company for home improvement consumers and contractors, shared her success with a group of colleagues at the International Builders Show. As she spoke about the rising cost of lumber, other senior executives nodded in commiseration.

She continued, "We heard complaints from contractors about being out of stock on items and about the length of our credit approval process. We needed to think more flexibly about how we did business without creating unmanageable disruptions within the company."

Andree inspired other Shoppers Square executives to focus on contractors. Many possibilities emerged. Executives purchased an electronic data interchange (EDI) system to alert manufacturers to replenish products when purchased, ensuring a well-stocked store. To offset the expense of the system, Shoppers Square partnered with 25 suppliers, offering rebates at the end of each quarter based on profits. The management team also replaced the long credit-approval processes with instant daily credit with payment due within 14 days. The introduction of the 7:00 AM Monday morning forums was the most exciting innovation. As contractors flocked into the stores for supplies, sales associates met them with coffee and pastries in exchange for their participation. During these 30-minute forums, useful information surfaced. For example, Andree found out that most contractors rarely purchase medium-sized product offerings, opting for large or small sizes. When she visited the 45 regional stores, she used these forums to solicit information and to educate the contractors about the building trade economy.

Though it is too early to predict the potential outcomes, Shoppers Square is receiving very positive feedback from contractors on company surveys. The Monday morning forums draw more people each month. Within six months, over 1,000 new contractor credit applications were approved. In addition, the average age of accounts receivable was reduced by 60 percent. Within the first three months of the changes, Shoppers Square eliminated over 5,000 SKUs, freeing up cash for other improvements.

As you develop relationships with your customers, you find out what is most important to them. You can also become their resource for up-to-date information about their industry and competitors. And, most customers want to see changes *now*.

## Anticipate Market Changes

When learning about changes in your industry, such as new entrants and disruptive technologies, how can you become flexible in dealing with them?

We are all retailers, no matter what we sell or services we offer. How quickly can your business change from a focus on your products to one focused on market needs and wants? For example, what would you do if you were Mattel and Bratz dolls hit the shelves? What would you do if the bank started foreclosing on your customer's properties because of the subprime market spillover? What would you do if Costco opened across the street and offered the same products that you sell at a cheaper price? What can you do *now*, before your customers say "too little, too late" as they move their shopping carts across the way?

Making incremental changes will not help you most of the time. Actually, incremental changes can frequently become an excuse to run in place, driving up costs and putting stress on your systems and people.

When potentially threatened with a new competitor, Mercy Hospital in Manhattan, Kansas, a small community hospital, responded flexibly with an effective approach. A new competitive Women's Clinic opened one block away and began offering parenting classes. A market-aware and persistent nurse practitioner at Mercy Hospital convinced the CEO and his management team to make radical changes and become a full-fledged community health center as soon as possible. Within weeks, the hospital began offering employee assistance programs, parenting classes, substance abuse education, free clinics two mornings per week, and a variety of community education programs. This hospital acted with speed and was not left in the dust for long.

Hallmark became Hallmark Entertainment. Disney added retail stores. Waldenbooks and Borders offered rewards cards providing a 5 percent discount with each purchase. Does this sound simple? Not necessarily. Staying ahead of the curve requires vigilant awareness of consumer trends and competitive moves. It can cost a great deal of money in marketing, sales, and product additions. It is especially important to be sure the changes coincide with other aspects of your strategy; otherwise, the approach will appear fragmented with a lack of integration. Changes may require significant shifts and modifications in an otherwise previously solid plan. The *Integration* PROFITS principle, discussed in the next chapter, addresses how your company can implement change using a cohesive and linked approach based on Fortune 100 principles that can save successful small and medium-sized companies time and expense.

Kreitman Associates, an accounts receivable company with revenues in 2008 of $3 million and employing 33 people, was unable to keep up with innovations in the field. The company did not have the money or capabilities to transform the business quickly. What did it do? David Kreitman found a new business opportunity, with Kreitman Associates adding value to an already successful outsourcing consortium by providing accounts receivable outsourcing and partnering with other companies that sold insurance and credit cards. The consortium shared benchmarking and market research data, becoming a one-stop-shopping experience for the customers who bought their products. All companies in the consortium profited. Within three months, Kreitman Associates increased revenues by 100 percent and hired 10 more people. How did David do it?

The secret of David's success was in clearly communicating his priorities to his staff and to his consortium partners.

## Communicate Priorities

David communicated in groups and with one person at a time. He announced the expected changes and his expectations for how the company would operate.

He also invited the new management team of the consortium and leaders from the consortium partner companies (suppliers and outsourcing companies) to speak with the staff directly.

In addition, David communicated to his customers and directed his employees to do the same. Account representatives notified customers immediately about the future changes, thanking them for their patronage and asking them to remain as customers. On follow-up surveys, customers stated they felt valued and respected by the account representative, who assured them that the customer could call the representative personally. As a result of these surveys, Kreitman assigned personal account representatives to each customer and provided the option of speaking with someone else if the customer's own representative was not available. This fostered a greater personal relationship between Kreitman and the customer. As previously stated (Chapter 5, *Obtain Vital Information*), though there are many functions you might wish to outsource, you should never outsource customer service. This is your key interface with your customer and an ongoing opportunity to strengthen your relationships.

Certainly there were customers who resisted the changes at Kreitman Associates. Anticipating this possibility, the new account representative training program addressed potential customer resistance and instructed representatives to ask challenging customers to speak with David Kreitman personally. Many times this resulted in increased customer retention and an even stronger relationship with the customer.

David Kreitman communicated clearly that customers were his company's number one priority, but saying it and implementing it are two different things. Successful implementation requires measuring the results of your actions effectively.

## Measure Effectively

David firmly believed that tying rewards to measures leads to accomplishing the company goals. During training sessions, instructors educated employees about essential profitability metrics. The depth of education for each metric was geared to specific job positions. Thus, appropriate measures for each employee position led to the likelihood for attaining success.

Each quarter, the management team reviewed the profitability metrics. Only those metrics directly affecting profitability mattered. For many companies, these are measures of customer service, expenses for servicing accounts, customer retention, new customer acquisition, and customer terminations. At Kreitman, each person in the company kept records for each metric, and these records became part of the quarterly review process.

Although individual account representatives and their teams received performance ratings for customer service, David also extended these ratings to all levels of the company. He believed that every person interacts with customers, including those customers within one's own organization to whom one handed off work.

Components of measuring performance include employee recognition and company celebrations of success.

## Celebrate Success

Celebration is the expression of appreciation for the valuable contributions of your employees. For example, an oral surgeon I know takes his 10 employees and their spouses to a Broadway show each Christmas season. He purchases orchestra seating and includes dinner at Mama Mia's in New York City before the show. Is this extravagant? Yes and no. For a few thousand dollars a year, the staff truly enjoys each other's company in a lavish setting. The evening reinforces company camaraderie and loyalty, rewarding the hard work accomplished daily in this successful practice.

## BE AN INFLUENCER

Influential people earn the admiration of others by going beyond mere communicating to modeling explicit behaviors of respect for those who work with and for them. Leading by influence means that you:

- *Know what you want and why*
- *Ferret out untruths*
- *Give up the one right way*

### Know What You Want and Why

As the company leader, you have already discovered gaps between what you want the company to accomplish and your current capabilities. You can anticipate most market trends and the needs and wants of your customers.

In your role as leader, you demonstrate the ability to set clear goals, prioritize expectations, and communicate these expectations effectively. You communicate well and often, keeping people apprised of ongoing situations and future considerations. You provide relevant time lines for work and make yourself available to answer questions. These actions are more important than ever in our current business environment of greater customer expectations and entitlements.

As the lead communicator, it is your responsibility to uncover erroneous assumptions that can stall and interfere with your peak profitability goals.

### Ferret Out Untruths

What do people in your company believe that may not be true? What can you do to inspire confidence in people's attitudes, skills and behaviors to increase your company's profitability? Are people fearful of a competitor who surpassed your revenues last quarter? Are they concerned about India, China and other emerging markets that may overtake your market share? What can you do when your employees believe that higher interest rates will undercut your ability to purchase the systems you require to run your business effectively? Most important, how do you help people understand that what is good for the company is best for them? Do you provide training to develop your employee's critical thinking skills? Do you encourage open dialogue for people to discuss inconsistencies or misconceptions with each other? Do you accede to your staff that there is more than one right way?

## Give Up *the* One Right Way

The effects of having only one right way can permeate all you do both inside and outside the company. The degree of autonomy you offer employees within your company for solving problems has a direct effect on how your employees interact with customers. How do you utilize the suggestions of your employees?

Mo Johnson, CEO of PackPlus, a $5 million packaging company, designs bottles and containers for pharmaceuticals. At his most recent meeting with a major distributor, Mo learned of new research showing that patients are more compliant when their physicians prescribe elongated pills than when taking small round pills.

Rob, one of Mo's employees, suggested that PackPlus update the design of its containers to better accommodate elongated pills. After a few hours of careful consideration, Mo, with Rob's assistance, reconfigured some of the PackPlus packaging. After reviewing the specifications with a CAD designer and graphics consultant, Mo only needed to make small modifications in the shape of the container throat and cap, and to reposition the labels. PackPlus could continue using its current production equipment. He further increased the company's capabilities by joining a new supply chain network that helped him speed delivery, reduce storage requirements, and improve logistics and inventory turnover overall. Because Mo was receptive to Rob's suggestion, PackPlus profited from a new opportunity instead of suffering a setback as manufacturers switched to the more popular pill shape.

There are other examples. Wal-Mart penetrated the grocery products industry. Stop & Shop did the same with banking services. What if Clairol did not market hair color to younger women or if the SUV was not designed for suburban families? All of these unusual choices came about because someone listened to an employee with a good idea.

## FOSTER INTERACTIVE COMMUNICATION

The world is getting flatter. That means the world appears smaller with less time to accomplish what we need to do and greater transparency about what we actually do. You can now find formerly proprietary information on the Internet and in other published sources. Even private companies that previously enjoyed anonymity find themselves chatted about online. However, information on the Internet is not always accurate. Your company's reputation and future profits can quickly be in jeopardy as a result of one or two disgruntled customers or employees who use the Internet as a forum to voice their displeasure.

Many companies proactively disarm concerns by establishing dialogue both within and outside the company by disclosing their business practices.

You can do this when you:

- *Create forums for dialogue*
- *Encourage customer/staff social networking*

It is important to establish dialogue, because chat groups and other consumer forums are offering many direct channels to our customers.

## Create Forums for Dialogue

Consumer channels provide the opportunity to inspire trust in your company by providing multiple types of forums. One company, ChatXY, targets first-time buyers of home and baby products, cars, and furniture for Generation X and Y shoppers. They offer biweekly opportunities for consumers to ask specific questions to the 28-year-old Generation Y consultant.

There are other Internet forums for companies that want to provide greater value to their existing customers who have share of wallet for new services within their category. One beauty salon now offers reciprocal arrangements for customers with a local health spa and with the YWCA for a small discounted fee when customers register online. Based on an Internet forum match, a local roofing company bought a franchise for newly designed gutters to supplement its offerings. A telephone call center operation began selling phones and wiring in addition to customer service.

## Encourage Customer/Staff Social Networking

Creating your own internal company forums both in person and on your intranet can be a positive communication tool within your business for sharing ideas, resources, and collaboration on projects. Few things are more empowering than listening and being listened to. New social networks show up on the Internet every day. There are networks for learning about any topic, such as Alltop, My3cents.com, Vault.com, and Digg. Twitter, Facebook, and LinkedIn are perhaps the most popular forums for personal and professional connections.

In our culture of expression and thirst for information, this new kind of networking works. People find it easy and fun to communicate on their computers. It is a shorter excursion to a computer chat room than making a phone call or walking down the hall. The important message is to provide an environment that encourages employee communication by creating the processes leading to information sharing.

## CREATE PROCESSES

As mentioned earlier, some people confuse positive flexibility—the creative, adaptive, and thoughtful responses to new circumstances—with uncontrolled flexibility, which is really chaos and lack of discipline. How can you alleviate most of the chaos in your business? A well-engineered process can address potential chaos and provide the knowledge that offers direction by considering the following actions:

- *Know what's expected*
- *Attend to details*
- *Play in the white space*

### Know What's Expected

People who know their industry and job scope well have better judgment than average when they consider making changes. This is primarily because they understand the expectations associated with these changes within the reality of the market. They know what changes are truly outside the box and devise contingency plans and communication vehicles for these challenges. They also know which changes are no big deal.

Andree Milivan, COO of Shoppers Square, had a strong grasp of her company's strategies and goals. She planned to employ most of the existing strategy in driving her new solution. Andree anticipated possible future challenges and knew why they might occur. As a result, she successfully put forth her new ideas with clear goals and objectives.

Though unexpected market shifts may disrupt these well-designed strategies, it is still important to have a plan. You should maintain flexibility and not always regiment yourself to strictly follow every detail. However, it is not a contradiction to say that a well-designed plan with specific details reminds you where you are going and demonstrates a well-grounded thinking process.

## Attend to Details

Andree at Shoppers Square attended to the details and demonstrated respect for everyone on the team who designed the original strategy. She prepared to tackle political, cultural, and technical opposition, while being accountable for her new plans. Along with suggested modifications in strategy, Andree addressed such key company functions as sales and operations. She offered specific solutions for greater flexibility in dealing with manufacturers by demonstrating knowledge of production, facilities, and warehouses, much to the appreciation of her peers. She had insights about payment strategies and was sensitive to the CFO's concerns.

Although extremely detail-oriented, Andree was actually setting the groundwork for greater creativity and flexible decision making. This became evident in the solutions that eventually became company policy when dealing with contractors and making it easier for the contractors to do business with Shoppers Square.

## Play in the White Space

Similar to Andree Milivan, David Kreitman, CEO of Kreitman Associates, also attended to details and remained true to his strategic vision, always vigilant to the strategic boundaries of his investors. He knew the limitations of his company's capabilities and the pool of his people's skills. Because he was master of these details, David could present acceptable changes in his strategy to his investment team, based on rethinking current resources, adding the capabilities of other companies in the consortium and projecting expected profitability improvements. He worked intensely with his own management team for three days, anticipating challenges to the new plans for change. Although the current strategy was only a few months old, David knew that time was of the essence and there was no point holding onto an outworn strategy—even if it was relatively new.

As part of a consortium, Kreitman forecasted higher margins based on projected reduced costs due to shared marketing, research and development, and many other pooled services. It was a win-win solution. David's focus on the strategic boundaries and his attention to details allowed his management team to play in the white space between those boundaries. David's analysis made sense and the investors wholeheartedly approved. The important takeaway is that David kept sight of his strategic direction and remained focused on profits. Joining the consortium was a modified strategy aligned to Kreitman Associates' committed vision.

Many companies create alliances and become part of consortia where partners share expenses that free up cash for more profitable solutions. In the case of Kreitman and his new consortium, their own customers started to do just that. By outsourcing areas outside their core capabilities, like accounts receivable, these customers gained the cash to extend their own core capabilities into new and exciting customer solutions.

## DO IT NOW

David Kreitman approached his investors quickly. He did not obsess and agonize over changing the strategy. When the consortium opportunity emerged, he jumped on it, not wanting to lose out to a competitor. Being clear about Kreitman Associates' direction and knowing that the consortium solution would be the profitable route inspired David to influence his investors with confidence. The following avenues guided his success and can guide you, too.

- *Know your direction*
- *Take action*
- *Experiment*
- *Get back on the horse*

Though the existing strategy for the company was in place for only three months, it was already outmoded. Unfortunately, too many companies wait out a bad strategy. They hang on and get hung up. When they decide to move on, precious time has already been lost and they lag behind competitors. Most never recover.

## Know Your Direction

Both Andree and David knew the direction set for the company. They knew the business's core capabilities, the available capital, and the time it would take to redesign processes. In both cases, the company's core capabilities and present processes supported the new strategic solution. Andree and David also had the confidence to work with the uncertainty of the market, knowing they had enough information and knowledge of the company to lead it through the market's ambiguity.

Sometimes a company's core capabilities do not address customer needs. In those cases, you will have to find a way to build or outsource capabilities and not hang on to outmoded internal strengths.

## Take Action

The best approach is to keep moving. Though you do not want to take action aimlessly, movement is good because you can discover ways to fine-tune your steps since the market provides feedback quickly. If you know your industry well, you do not want to lose market share to the competition, and you can make educated guesses without taking overwhelming risks. You do not want to read about another company's success using ideas that you already considered. If you attend to the details, know your limitations, and have the important processes in place, your actions will be a first step towards greater profits. Once you take action, the flaws will surface and if you pay attention, you can correct your course.

Initially, Andree actually lost money by reducing the product line at Shoppers Square. The contractors stated they only needed large and small quantities of most products, so the company eliminated over 5,000 SKUs of stock. The lost money resulted from the reduced revenues from do-it-yourselfers consumers who usually bought numbers of products between those extremes. Do-it-yourselfers provided 20 percent less revenue than contractors across every category, so the loss of market share and revenue from them was insignificant over the long run when compared with the increased revenue from contractors.

Andree used the opportunity to become even more aggressive in targeting contractors. Revenues from contractors were up 25 percent after two quarters, reinforcing Andree's assumption that the system now realigned in-stock products to meet their forecast needs. Ironically, Shoppers Square now utilized less warehouse storage due to the EDI system, which Andree fought for in her negotiations for the new strategy. By taking action and experimenting, Andree found the future profits for Shoppers Square.

## Experiment

Experimenting develops resiliency. Sometimes you fail and you have the chance to dust yourself off and try again. A marketing company targeting corporate brand managers for e-mail alerts found after a few months that brand managers did not respond to its trial subscription offer. After taking some risks and experimenting with other companies, the marketers found that their true target group was direct mail companies. Tolerating risks and taking the plunge strengthens your confidence.

## Get Back on the Horse

The reality show *Dancing with the Stars* is a very successful business for ABC Television because it taps the consumer's identification with the value-add of getting back on the horse. Twelve celebrities with no dance experience use the confidence and resiliency they have already developed in their individual areas of expertise to learn a new skill—ballroom dancing. Throughout

10 weeks, the viewer follows the trials, tribulations, joys, successes, and frustrations as the stars bear the judgment of the experts and vie for the trophy. Each week a pair is eliminated and those who remain demonstrate astounding resiliency as they tackle new dances and perform in front of millions of viewers and voters. Although each star wants to win the trophy, they all agree that the effort, commitment, and persistence build resiliency in their character. When asked afterward, they all say they value the resiliency above anything else they learned. ABC highlighted a winning consumer trend with this programming.

## SUMMARY

Successfully adapting to market changes can accelerate within a culture of *flexibility*. We examined the attributes of flexibility for leaders who champion change. These leaders can identify their expected results, anticipate market changes, communicate priorities, measure effectively, and celebrate success.

Next, we looked at the connection between a company entrepreneur and an influencer within your company. You know what you want and why. You can ferret out untruths and give up the belief in the one right way. You can foster interactive communication by creating forums for dialogue both within and outside your company and by encouraging customer/staff social networking.

Creating processes based on the company's most essential parameters provides you with the vital information to identify customer expectations, attend to details, and play in the white space, creating new and flexible solutions for your customers.

Chapter 5, *Obtain Vital Information*, was a reminder that you rarely have all the information you want for taking action. At some point, you simply have to "do it now." When you know your direction, you can move forward and let go of an outdated strategy. You can take action, experiment, and get back on the horse. The next step is integrating all your actions within all functions of your company.

## QUESTIONS AND ACTIONS FOR YOUR BUSINESS PROFITS

- Select an initiative with the potential for huge profits for your company—although there are significant risks. This can be a current project or one you think about often.
  - → Champion this project, select a project team, clarify the expected results, and communicate the priorities throughout your company.
  - → Measure the progress and momentum of the project after three months.
  - → Determine what worked and what did not work.
- Using the preceding initiative or another one, identify the untrue assumptions that may exist about this initiative within your company.
  - → Create a forum for employees to brainstorm how this project can be successful.
  - → Encourage people to challenge the "one right way" solutions.
- Continuing with the same initiative (or another one), design workable processes within three key functional areas (operations, sales, marketing).
  - → Request volunteers to join cross-functional teams for each new process.
  - → Allow each team to determine roles, responsibilities, and accountabilities for their process.

| P | Position Only for Growth |
|---|---|
| R | Reality |
| O | Obtain Vital Information |
| F | Flexibility |
| I | Integration |
| T | Test and Revise |
| S | Steering the Company |

**CHAPTER 7**

# Integration

> *Beaver: Gee, it seems that everything is connected to everything else, isn't it Dad?*
>
> *Ward: Just about, Beav.*
>
> —Leave it to Beaver

*Integration* is a competitive advantage for successful small and medium-sized companies. When all parts of the company work together, *integration* creates a whole that is more successful in achieving profitability than the sum of its individual components. With fewer people and less bureaucracy, smaller companies can achieve the advantage of integration, along with speed, cost, adaptability, employee participation, focus, and efficiency, more easily than a Fortune 100 can.

The principle, *Integration* is the lockstep approach for aligning and fostering congruency within your company. It is the PROFITS principle that focuses your attention on linking your company's strategic intent to specific goals and ignoring everything else. This adds cohesiveness to your business and accelerates profitability.

**117**

## INTEGRATION—HOW THE PIECES FIT TOGETHER

You are profitable. Feedback from your customers is positive. Life is good.

Yet, you know you could advance your company to the next level if you only knew how. The more success you achieve, the more this elusive element haunts you.

What else can you do? When you focus on *Integration*, you can change your thinking. First, decide if you want to expand your business. This can mean adding new projects, taking on greater responsibility, and/or hiring additional employees. This is a way to grow your profits, yet not the only route. You can also become more profitable by carefully examining your existing business functions and integrating them effectively. Overlooked frequently as an indispensable business gem, integration will frequently boost your business with less expense and less effort than entrepreneurs realize. The following actions will help you achieve this frequently ignored business treasure trove of profitability.

- *Scrutinize your business functions*
- *Interrelate metrics*
- *Be a cultural anthropologist*
- *Simplify your strategic intent*

Peekaboo Child, a $75 million company based in Geneva, Switzerland, with 180 employees worldwide and profits steadily increasing by approximately 10 percent per year, illustrates the theme of *Integration*.

Peekaboo Child manufactures a five-piece baby stroller, unparalleled in the industry for safety and design, with developmentally appropriate attachment options as the child grows. While Peekaboo Child's flexibility and creativity are hallmarks of its success in a competitive market, the company's vision and mission are not negotiable. Without exception, all new products and enhancements must improve the existing stroller; as a result, the company is focused, coordinated, and well integrated.

Peekaboo Child's discipline begins with its cross-functional management team, which cascades to cross-functional teams in each of five regions. Though the primary focus is selling, each team includes representation from other functional areas, including finance, operations, development, and marketing. Each team member is a salesperson first with functional expertise. This philosophy ensures sales accountability across the company and breaks down old functional silos such as operations versus sales or engineering versus technology, allowing Peekaboo Child to thrive as an integrated company within a culture of trust.

Team members identify sales opportunities and the person with sales expertise is responsible for qualifying and managing each account. The team uses weekly meetings to brainstorm new approaches to providing better service for both trade customers and consumers. The weekly agenda may include design modifications suggested by customer feedback. Customers attend monthly focus groups and the team makes decisions about color, fabric, and other related information with input from customers. The Peekaboo Child team obtains priceless learning about customers and their purchasing habits during these sessions. This information helps them remain fully focused on the customers' needs and wants.

The team's finance specialist evaluates options for outsourcing design and engineering tasks. The operations specialist monitors the supply chain cycle, and others track competitive stroller sales. Cross-functional teams become repositories of vital information that Peekaboo Child taps for remaining customer-focused and operating optimally as a well-integrated company.

How well is your business integrated? What are some ways for you to find out?

## SCRUTINIZE YOUR BUSINESS FUNCTIONS

When did you last examine your logistics department, equipment processing, human resources, order fulfillment center, customer service—and order taking areas to see if they worked, well together? Doing this routinely improves your ability to:

- *Recognize mismatched pieces*
- *Reorient toward customers and profits*
- *Discover what's missing*
- *Find the distractions*

Scope creep tends to take over in organizations, causing loss of focus. Projects not considered strategic may begin to flourish. Refusing unrelated projects and processes helps you remain free of unnecessary clutter in your business.

### Recognize Mismatched Pieces

Every step forward builds on what is already in place. We sometimes find pieces here and there, discovering they never really fit at all.

When Carla graduated from a prestigious business school five years ago, her plan was to redefine the fashion industry. In this "flat world" culture, she was going straight to the top, defying years of tradition and refusing to "play the nice girl who follows the rules."

Carla, like most of us, did some things well and others not so well. She designed a revolutionary undergarment that she knew would appeal to women all over the world. Carla patented her product, Away With the Underbelly and found a manufacturer in China that presented her with inventory of 10,000 garments. Approaching buyers from top department stores and boutiques, Carla surprised them with her disarming innocence upon arriving unannounced at their offices. More often than not, Carla's method worked and within six months, Away With the Underbelly was flying off the shelves of luxury purveyors such as Neiman Marcus and Henri Bendel.

Carla's problems began when she did not continue marketing Away With the Underbelly in a broader market.

Carla heeded the advice of her designer friend, Sophie, who had little business experience. Sophie told her to "ride the wave" of Away With the Underbelly and develop new product lines as soon as possible. Though Carla knew she was not ready to take on more, she wanted to be successful "right now" and began selling the Skinny Belt.

Carla did not have the time or desire to research the market for the Skinny Belt. She relied on her China manufacturer to choose the materials and she guessed on pricing. Now she had two product lines and did not know how to differentiate the star product from the loose cannon.

Carla did not pay attention to her accountant's advice when he cautioned her to slow down. She dismissed him, thinking, "I know how conservative accountants are."

The Skinny Belt was a complete failure. Within six months, the company was in the red and Carla lost her focus. The product line that did well when it stood alone suffered an enormous setback. Buyers associated the Skinny Belt and Away With the Underbelly and sold them together as a package. With no real connection between the two garments, buyers' interest vanished for both.

### Skinny Belt Resurrected

With her Skinny Belt in hand, Carla finally got the message. She withdrew it from stores and began to focus a chic marketing strategy to bring Away With the Underbelly back to the marketplace.

Five years later, Carla's business is a success and she is again contemplating a new product line. In the past six months, she piloted a new undergarment in her most successful markets with a marketing campaign that highlights the patented materials used in both garments and builds upon Carla's accomplishments in the fashionable undergarment sector. Projected sales based on the experience of the test market appear excellent.

### How Did This Happen?

The first few principles of PROFITS highlight Carla's mistakes. She created a top-notch product that sold well, but she had the common illusion that one good product makes a business. Her excitement and inward focus on her company obstructed her view of *reality* until loss of profitability affected her premier brand. Carla did not have a *position for growth* or a strategy.

As Carla rode the wave on Away With the Underbelly, she jumped in with the Skinny Belt without market analysis or researching her potential customers to *obtain vital information*. She failed to create a business or marketing plan and she did not test-market her products before investing her assets. Carla did not build *flexible* processes. By committing to a manufacturer in China and going on gut feelings, she was on the road to financial devastation. Worst of all, she was not aware of the urgent need to *integrate* all areas of her business.

Fortunately, Carla got her business back on track. Most entrepreneurs in Carla's situation do not recover their losses. Worse, they are never quite sure about what went wrong.

Sustaining and growing a successful business requires careful planning and analysis for integrating new product lines. Next, we look at Doug's experience as entrepreneur of an insurance company and some of the decisions he made in growing his business.

Doug's five-year-old company was thriving until he added small business insurance to his current line of individual life and property products. Like Carla, Doug jumped into an area without sufficient preparation and knowledge. Doug did not have the financial expertise or capital within his company to add and market this new line of product. He was not credible with the customers who expected sophisticated knowledge of their small business needs. The new business simply did not integrate well with his existing company.

Similar to Carla, Doug did not consider the effect that his new business focus had on current customers. For example, to reduce expenses he eliminated resources that he considered to be frills, such as coffee, pastries, newspapers and financial magazines he offered to customers as they waited in his reception area. Though these cost almost $2,000 per month, the niceties added warmth to Doug's business approach.

Ultimately, Doug's funding sources dried up and his partner left the company. Doug eventually had to give up his business and now operates an accounting function for a brokerage firm.

Although he enjoys his new career, he wishes he did things differently.

## Reorient Toward Customers and Profits

You are most successful as an entrepreneur when you enjoy fulfilling your customers' desires. This satisfaction permeates all aspects of your business, including your communications with customers and staff. Fulfilling customers' desires is why we stay in business and what makes us profitable. Developing relationships with customers and asking for their feedback is an inexpensive investment for improving your business. As an entrepreneur, you can speak with many customers personally, learning how they perceive your company and what their expectations are for the products they want.

Speaking with customers provides information you can use to tailor your customer solutions—making it easier for them to do business with you. Your business becomes effortless when you are in step with what your customers want. As you adapt your business, you create an interlocking value chain between your customers and yourself. Sometimes customers invite you into their businesses for you to learn more about their unique needs. This offers you an opportunity to create profits together. And you can do this whether they invite you or not. The information you receive from or about customers can help you commingle your business processes, although it is not always apparent that this is happening. All you need to do is choose to operate your business with this mind-set. Think about how you can position your business to save money for your customers and pass these savings on to their customers. If you continually think about integrating and linking your business with your customers' businesses, most of your processes will start aligning with this objective.

One method to improve your business integration is to create cross-functional teams within your business. Teams comprised of members with different functional expertise work together on customer projects. These teams are most effective when given a clear mission—to be collaborative partners with others in your business and with those along the customer value chain. Peekaboo Child, the opening case in this chapter, continuously builds this capability with great success.

In summary, the vital information received about the customer is the most important information you have for saving them money and creating profitable growth for you.

## Discover What's Missing

When you are working hard on a project, dancing as fast as you can, it is difficult to stop and evaluate your performance. This is especially true when you are striving to resolve issues and meet deadlines. One more bit of information may be one too many. Yet, taking the time to evaluate your work can bring overlooked items to light while preventing problems and accelerating project completion.

Consider a regional home goods store that lost its edge by concentrating on the competition and missing important information about its customers and processes.

Senior management engaged a consultant to research the competition but did not disclose the project to middle management. Word about the project leaked out though, and soon rumors began to spread that the company was in trouble. With no communication from top management, employees decried the "culture of secrets."

Worried employees began to work at cross-purposes, hurting the company's reputation among customers. Even so, during the three-month project, none of the senior managers suggested pausing to assess the impact of the project and their own inaction on the company. The staff grew increasingly resentful and the company took a turn for the worse, all because management *told* them what they needed to do differently, without explaining or asking for their input. Inevitably, downsizing and restructuring followed.

It is easy to identify the management team's mistakes. Sadly, the executives did not realize what was happening because they dismissed employee discouragement and panic—completely missing the root problems. Had they assessed the project and the troubles it engendered, management could have obtained invaluable information about customers and internal processes. They could have redesigned and integrated processes by adding flexible approaches for customer ease. With better-integrated information from several sources, the company would have discovered what was missing and suffered less.

Executives of another large retail company reviewed operations of four distribution centers to determine the most efficient and profitable solutions for transporting new products to stores. They considered the cost of transportation and subsequent operating margins for several options.

One pivotal issue surfaced. The merchandise advertised in flyers did not arrive at stores in time for the sales events and the stores lost customers. Vendors shipped slowly and the company had no recourse due to their contractual agreements. Stores did not have logistics systems to track products received or purchased. Installing new systems would not alleviate the difficulty because employees lacked the knowledge to work with complex data and sophisticated computer systems. Management's solution was to replace regional warehouses with centralized just-in-time production and delivery. Top management considered designing new regional systems and prudently decided that the culture change would be disruptive and outweigh the benefits at this time.

The difference between this retail company and the earlier example is that this company's management assessed several contingencies and reached a logical and integrated solution based on knowledge and critical thinking. The managers in this example avoided various distractions as they analyzed distribution. Rather than focus exclusively on issues within each region, the managers kept their resolve to focus on the larger company.

## Find the Distractions

Distractions often result from lack of information, conflicting information, or normal shifts in a changing environment. Distractions are not always negative. The key is to recognize those distractions that can fragment your priorities. These drain precious time and energy you can apply to important projects that integrate well with your strategy and lead to higher profitability.

Jon, a product manager, brainstormed with his team about new products for SteelParts Inc., a steel accessories company, unaware that senior managers recently decided to focus only on marketing existing products for the next year. Lacking this knowledge, Jon spent almost a month developing strategic and marketing plans for new products and looking forward to senior management's approval. The plans never made it to the management team's agenda, and Jon felt as if he wasted his time.

When you examine your business frequently and communicate well, distractions become apparent quickly and you can address them before they cause a crisis. Analyzing the interrelationships among your financial measures helps you stay on track.

## INTERRELATE METRICS

When metrics interrelate, business goals link and the company remains focused. Activities synchronize, even when your company has several divisions. The following actions ensure these relationships:

- *Correlate measures*
- *Build internal consistency*
- *Demonstrate cause and effect*
- *Connect measures and rewards*

### Correlate Measures

Do the measures you use relate? In other words, do measures of overall company goals cascade down into measures for specific activities and products? Are you familiar with the measures that build into profitability?

The management of the home goods store reviewed bottom-line sales for the company each week. Due to lower quarterly revenues, the company embarked on a program of deep discounts, cost cutting, vendor discounts, and staff reductions. Management did not consider differences in each store's performance or store requirements. Similarly, some managers reviewed categories but not individual products. For example, the small electrical appliances category performed at a 20 percent profit margin. Management did not look at individual products and was not aware that within the slow cooker category, which enjoyed a 32 percent profit margin, one model of a well-known, good-quality brand had a very high return rate. This product, advertised intensively because of its bells and whistles, brought traffic into the stores. Failing to analyze returns represented a lost opportunity for management to find out what customers did not like and how this experience might affect future shopping behavior.

One way to obtain vital information is to classify products into cost centers—a best practice utilized by many Fortune 100 companies. You document all costs for each product, rather than utilizing only balance sheets and other income and cash statements that may lack adequate detail. It is important to define costs and expenses for each product and service line using common terminology and measures, thereby operating your business as a whole comprised of component parts that tell a consistent, well-integrated financial story. This internal consistency is your best assurance of a cohesive and *accurate* picture of your profitability.

## Build Internal Consistency

Do you receive frequent industry and company sales reports? What is your cash position each week? What is your quarterly inventory turnover? What is the variance for key metrics compared with last quarter? Are some products cannibalizing others? What are the daily production rates? What are the weekly financial trends? Which vendors are meeting goals? How quickly do accounts payable become accounts receivable for every product you sell? Does every employee in the company know these statistics? Are you measuring what is important—or what is easy?

The key is to be sure you can link *all* your measures and trace them back to a specific product or service cost. Review pricing, fixed and variable costs, interest rates, and a variety of expense ratios. Thoroughly analyze all relationships and discrepancies, viewing them as themes that can expose hidden treasures of greater profitability.

### Demonstrate Cause and Effect

The cause of a problem is not always evident. Go back to the previous example of the small electrical appliances department in the home goods store.

In some stores, vendors did not get products to the store in time for an advertised sale. If management had metrics demonstrating the performance for each vendor and projected the lost sales, they could make knowledgeable decisions about possibly changing vendors, revising advertisements and determining realistic time lines. Quite possibly, the vendors might not have enough lead time. The printing company may be missing time lines in the production of the flyers. Associates in the stores may not know that the products did not arrive because they received 12 mislabeled boxes and did not have the time to unpack them on the day the boxes arrived on the delivery truck.

The worst-case scenario is that customers buy the products from your competitor when you are out of stock. It is critical to know and *not assume* why sales are lower than expected or why profit margins are lower than projected. Without accuracy of cause and effect, you cannot solve the problems of your business.

You also need to be sure that you are actually measuring profitability, which is the vital information that matters. Then you can work backwards to find the component measures. Profitability measures include return on investments, return on assets, and various margin and operating metrics.

Fortune 100 companies frequently demonstrate cause and effect with a balanced scorecard approach. The company defines metrics relating to the customer, internal processes, and organizational learning to supplement financial measures, providing a variety of metrics encompassing the entire business. This makes good sense because your company's health includes more than financial measures, which are lagging indicators reporting past events. The balanced scorecard is a well-integrated business report card.

## Connect Measures and Rewards

What you measure influences behavior. An example is a team that agrees on its own priorities for allocating resources. The team then establishes specific targets (or outcome measures) for accountability that measures the efficient use of these resources. These outcome measures directly affect employee pay. Though this process takes time and trust, the results are generally excellent for companies engaging in this practice.

The following example illustrates a company culture where teams determine their priorities and measures. Observing and interpreting how your people work together will convey indicators for improving integration within your company.

## BE A CULTURAL ANTHROPOLOGIST

Bill Gore opened the doors of W. L. Gore Associates in 1958 with his wife Vieve. The privately owned chemical company with 8,000 associates earns over $2 billion in revenue annually. Multidisciplinary teams share project responsibility and employees are encouraged to take personal initiative for all company activities. Well-integrated functional teams create projects and leadership emerges once projects begin. Teams select their leaders based on the knowledge and talents of team members. Employee retention and employee satisfaction are high because of the teams' autonomy and decision-making accountability.

Can your company match this remarkable growth and way of operating? Use the following practices to discover your own answers:

- *Connect to company history*
- *Decode norms and values*

- *Decipher information centers*
- *Verify accountability*

## Connect to Company History

If you started the company, recall your earliest days. What are the messages you articulated to employees, customers, media, friends, and professional organizations about your company? Did you operate with rules, a vision statement, processes, and goals? How did you assign work? How did you determine what to sell? How did you evaluate work? Did you have a strategy and a business plan? What did you expect from your employees, customers, investors, and other stakeholders? How did you communicate within your company? How did you treat employees? What was your management style?

You may still operate as you did when you started your company. That may be positive or negative. W. L. Gore Associates operates today much as it did in the 1960s—with astounding results. The point is that you set the stage years ago for how others perceive your company now. Earlier practices also influence how you currently operate your company.

As you think about how your company operates today, you will want to decode employee behavior, especially management behavior. Find clues to discover what pivotal events of the past may influence your business practices today.

## Decode Norms and Values

People in your company share a sense of purpose based on the messages they receive from you over time. These messages may be subtle, yet have a powerful effect. They shape how people work with each other and with customers. The messages are your showcase to the world.

Any culture, including that of your company, is deeply rooted in beliefs and values that members internalize. These values are the daily norms for what is and is not acceptable. That is why it is important for you to understand the underlying norms of your company. Few people operate as lone rangers, and the norms pertain to your entire business.

*When beliefs and values exist with tacit agreement for a long time, there is little to challenge. Violations of norms that grow out of cultural values tend to result in pressure to conform and organizational inertia can set in.*

The PROFITS principle, *Steering the Company* (Chapter 9) further exemplifies the importance of culture, norms and values within your business. Next, we explore how company norms and processes aid people to work together for business integration.

### Decipher Information Centers

Every business has communication hubs. People know the informal channels where they can find information. The three main categories of information are communication, advice, and trust. Communication connects people to one another to share what they hear and know. This helps get things done when formal structures are too slow and inefficient. The advice network connects people who turn to one another to seek counsel, obtain technical answers, and solve specific problems. It is more than mere communication. The trust center connects people who are willing to share sensitive information with one another. This is the highest level of communication.

It is in your best interest to uncover and map these hubs to learn how information travels through your company. Though some entrepreneurs may feel threatened by the perceived power of these information centers, they can serve as your best allies if your employees think of you as trustworthy and respectful.

### Verify Accountability

Everyone in your company needs to be accountable. Bill Gore began to build accountability in his chemical company from the day it opened its doors. When employees allocate resources and determine their target goals, accountability is clear. When rewards and pay link to these accountabilities, you have dependable employees. If your company has a traditional structure with managers setting goals, you may want to revisit your reward, measurement, and compensation systems.

You may need to clarify roles and responsibilities. This becomes even more complicated when you outsource or form alliances with other companies. In that case, it is also important to learn about the cultures of your partner companies and for you and your partners to agree to the accountabilities.

*It is interesting to note that culture and accountability differences are the most common reason for failures of mergers and acquisitions.*

One way of ensuring accountability is to clearly articulate and simplify your strategic intent, which confirms that all stakeholders and employees comprehend your message.

## SIMPLIFY YOUR STRATEGIC INTENT

Strategic intent is not your strategy or mission. Strategic intent identifies how you, the owner of a successful and profitable business, define your business's purpose. As you continue to link all parts of your business, it becomes easier to articulate, apply, and integrate your strategic intent within the whole company. To achieve strategic intent:

- *Clarify key constituencies*
- *Reinforce priorities*
- *Link your systems*
- *Convey consistency*

You probably defined constituencies when you started your company. These may change, and it is important to be aware of each group.

### Clarify Key Constituencies

Most businesses have at least four key constituencies. These are customers, suppliers, employees, and managers. Other constituencies may include a board of directors, community leaders, and others pertinent to your business. For the needs of each essential constituency, your business requires different core processes. As you review your constituencies, they each provide criteria for the design of your business. For each stakeholder you will want to evaluate the strength of your relationship and determine your expectations of one another.

The following core processes address customer requirements: production processes, service-delivery processes, new product development, and supporting technology development capabilities. For suppliers you will need quality and inspection, ordering, payment, material handling, and production planning systems. Employees require work design, information, appraisal, and reward systems. They also need training/development and compensation/benefits mechanisms. Your managers require planning, budgeting, measurement, and information systems. These are some minimum essentials. Of course, your list for your business can be much longer.

## Reinforce Priorities

Everyone in your company needs to know the company's priorities. When this is not the case, people work at cross-purposes, draining time and energy. Ideally, each employee attends meetings that highlight strategic priorities. Your role as CEO is to train all your employees to articulate the company expectations with accuracy.

It is important for managers to train employees in how the company and its systems work, including how their job responsibilities coincide with those of others in the company. These dialogues can take place in training sessions or in other company venues to educate employees about the ways company systems link.

## Link Your Systems

Systems establish procedures for organizations in allocating resources and monitoring the use of these resources. There are at least three systems in every well-functioning company. The first one is the information system, which uses vital information as a source of integration for understanding trends and patterns within an industry or market. Measures directly coincide with the information needed.

People systems recognize the importance of human assets. Many buisness leaders say, "People are our most important asset." This can be an abstract cliché. I will talk more about defining and respecting people assets later (Chapter 11, *People Processes*), as well as about ways to measure human capital productivity.

The third system refers to capital and investments. Best practices in this area use a value-based approach to determine funding for projects and initiatives. Again, appropriate measures to control these resources are essential.

A franchise business in Sweden honed its competitive advantage by linking systems using information differentiation. At point of sale, the company collected data on customer purchasing activity and demographics. Corporate headquarters, local stores and suppliers received continuous updates and analyses of the data, including best-selling items, items that lost or gained popularity, weather conditions at the times of purchases, product availability on shelves three hours prior to delivery, and ways to adjust upcoming shipments. There were estimates and forecasts for each store. Store managers learned to interpret and utilize this information in training seminars and on the job. As a result, average daily sales per store in Sweden were 30 percent higher than stores double their size in the United States.

Some companies consider human resources expenses as capital investments for their business. An automotive company expenses labor as a fixed rather than variable expense because it refuses to consider employees as overhead. Another automotive company shares tasks with labor and management, avoiding friction in a unionized environment. The United Auto Workers (UAW) union agreed to this with favorable results.

Investments in corporate universities, averaging $1,500 or more per employee in many Fortune 100 companies demonstrate the importance of developing and respecting human capital. Investing in training generally results in higher employee retention and is many times indicative of other employee considerations.

Even within our present world culture of frequent job changes, your investment in employee training is an investment in our world economy.

Your company's actions regarding important business systems express essential company messages about your best practices and are important in operating a consistent, integrated business.

### Convey Consistency

Similar to reinforcing priorities, conveying consistency emphasizes your company's commitment to its strategic intent. Along with your priorities, a consistent message highlights what your company stands for. Think about why you started your business. What did you hope to achieve? Whom did you want to serve? What is the heart and soul of your business, without which you would not want to continue your business? This is the message you want employees to live daily, both in and out of the office.

### SUMMARY

*Integration* focuses on designing a well-coordinated, reality-based company. You examined your company, looking for mismatched pieces, reorienting toward customers and profits, discovering what may be missing, and finding the distractions that exhaust your time and energy.

Next, you reviewed the interrelationships among your profitability metrics, correlating the types of measures you use to build internal consistency. You associated cause-and-effect connections between your metrics and learned the benefits of linking measures with rewards. As a cultural anthropologist, you learned the importance of comprehending the history, norms, and current values that underlie the behavior within your company—helping you decipher where the business information networks exist that verify the critical areas of accountability.

You then had the opportunity to revisit and simplify your strategic intent. This led to clarifying your key constituencies, reinforcing priorities, linking your systems, and conveying consistent company messages.

You are well on your way to a continuously profitable and well-integrated business within a constantly changing and uncertain environment. Next, you will have the opportunity to apply another best practice that many Fortune 100 companies follow, *Test and Revise*. This ensures your ongoing focus for a committed company purpose.

## QUESTIONS AND ACTIONS FOR YOUR BUSINESS PROFITS

- What areas of your business fit together?
  - → On a piece of paper, draw a circle and label it "customer." Outside the circle, list your company's functions (i.e., finance, operations, marketing, etc.) and list how each function serves your customer.
  - → List your key initiatives and daily activities. Determine if these are interrelated and if you can stop doing any of them.
- What are your key metrics and how do they interrelate?
  - → How do you measure your company's profitability?
  - → How do your key metrics provide the vital information for you and your customers for sustaining profitable growth and competitive advantage?
- What are the norms and values that guide behavior within your business?
  - → In a group forum, discuss with your staff how these underlying norms affect how your company operates.
  - → Determine whether your staff has the vital information for accountability in their work.
- Clearly state your strategic intent at a staff meeting.
  - → Ask staff members to identify your key constituencies.
  - → As a group, list the processes and expectations for each of these constituencies.

| P | Position Only for Growth |
|---|---|
| R | Reality |
| O | Obtain Vital Information |
| F | Flexibility |
| I | Integration |
| T | Test and Revise |
| S | Steering the Company |

**CHAPTER 8**

# Test and Revise

*If you don't like what you're doing you can always pick up your needle and move to another groove.*

—Timothy Leary

hough simple in concept, most entrepreneurs struggle to *Test and Revise* their business strategies and plans. Generally, this best practice is easier for Fortune 100 company executives who may have experienced humbling lessons with profit and revenue losses.

Most of their distressing experiences occur because of the scope creep discussed earlier. Scope creep arises when we allow distractions to find their way into our strategies. Offenders masquerade as interesting and tempting new projects and possibilities. Large-company executives *Test and Revise* their strategies, goals, and objectives in formal review processes in an effort to sidestep common distractions. Reviews often require a significant investment of time, yet the rewards and damage control they offer pay off richly.

The principle *Test and Revise*, the "T" in PROFITS, gives you the opportunity to excel as a leader by reaffirming and refining your original vision of your company.

Some best practices included in *Test and Revise* are:

- *Lead for excellence*
- *Question it all*
- *Reassess your strategy*
- *Continue to review*

Environmental Inc's CEO, Melanie (Chapter 2, *PROFITS*; Chapter 3, *Position Only for Growth*), learned the value of the *Test and Revise* process. GreenSoap Company, one of the subsidiaries, grew profitability this year, achieving 11% profits by modifying some its operating processes for greater efficiency. With a sales force of 38 people in the United States, three in Israel, and one each in France, Germany, Italy, England, and Portugal, Greensoap sold concentrated, environmentally safe green soap to commercial cleaning enterprises at $15.99 per container.

When GreenSoap was midway through its five-year strategic plan, Melanie revisited it because she feared the business was veering out of control. With fast growth and unexpected demand in Europe, GreenSoap now also faced competition in emerging markets. She viewed the current business as fragmented and worried that her company was becoming a ship without a rudder at the mercy of the weather. Overall, she perceived her role as reactive and she reluctantly hired additional salespeople and searched for global suppliers.

But Melanie's business was actually in good shape. When I visited her, we reviewed the business's strategic intent, financial situation, and internal operations, as well as data on the global environmental cleaning industry. We discovered that GreenSoap had adequate working capital for sustaining additional hiring and inventory. However, her accounting processes were making it difficult for customers to pay Melanie on time.

Turning her attention to slow deliveries, Melanie retained a logistics specialist to scope out the most efficient container carrier and transport routes to expedite overseas shipments.

She gave her human resources director a budget to get expert help in designing a sales training program and writing descriptions for every job in the company, including cross-functional roles. The need for better cooperation between teams became apparent during the mapping of cross-functional roles. For example, while the sales area had responsibility for closing a deal, the operations area determined how and when the customer would take delivery. It was critical, therefore, for sales and operations to work together closely. Melanie ensured this by inviting all employees to attend briefings on business deals valued at $20,000 or more.

Clarity of roles and coordination of activities resulted in less stress and greater operational efficiency for her business. With a little research, Melanie implemented new software and streamlined accounting procedures. In only three months, approvals and payments each accelerated by 10 days. These relatively small changes allowed Melanie to regain confidence as a leader who was in control of her business once again.

Melanie refocused the company on garnering more business in the United States, where GreenSoap was already successful. Thus, her strategic intent remained the same. Melanie realized that a successful global business overseas would require the commitment of significant time and money. She did not want the obligation of learning new markets, finding suppliers, and dealing with overseas competitors. Although she maintained a sales presence in Europe and Israel, Melanie's overseas customers sought her out through their contacts in the United States. She did not choose to pursue this market actively.

The new briefing meetings that Melanie held continued to serve as an open dialogue for exchanging ideas and learning what worked and what didn't. This inspired best practices and organized planning for future projects. As a result, the *Test and Revise* principle was integral to GreenSoap's best practices.

Melanie developed leadership excellence by reassessing her actions and committing to her strategic intent.

## LEAD FOR EXCELLENCE

You now run a business with satisfied customers and profits. Most of your business works well. As you *test and revise*, you have the opportunity to take your business to the next level of excellence when you:

- *Discover all perspectives*
- *Attend to details*

The stakeholders within your business—customers, employees, investors, and others—may look at your company with differing points of view. Each one is important to consider.

### Discover All Perspectives

Jordan Clemens owns and operates Clemens Boatworks, a $15 million company located in Massachusetts. Clemens recently built a custom sailboat for Jacques Anderson, owner of a private asset management company in Boston, an attractive man who is six feet five inches tall, with long legs and a slender build.

Jacques respected Jordan's reputation as a fine craftsman and asked Jordan to design and build a sailboat for him. Jordan designed Jacques' new 45-foot sailboat with the utmost care. Built with sensitivity to Jacques' height, the boat sports high railings for his comfort in maneuvering the sails. The seat height is five inches above standard specifications, and customized specifically for Jacques.

Jacques was extremely impressed when he first saw the boat; but he returned to Clemens Boatworks three weeks after taking delivery and described the discomfort his weekend guests experienced. They had difficulty crewing the boat with him because of the high railings. One man had to stand on his toes to reach the hardware on the mast as he pulled up the jib, since the hardware was customized to Jacques' height. Jacques further explained that accommodating for his height was already a way of life for him. Although he appreciated the boat's modifications, they created distress for his visitors.

The next day, Jordan Clemens went aboard *Feisty Face*, Jacques' new boat. He immediately realized that his narrow focus on Jacques precluded the consideration of other perspectives, including the people who sailed with him.

### Why Does This Matter to You?

As an entrepreneur, you set the tone for your company. Your customers do not exist in a vacuum. Your ability to expand your thinking and actions for seeing the world through your customers' eyes increases the quality of information you have for satisfying the desires of existing and potential customers.

Ask yourself the following questions: What are *all* of the relevant perspectives? What importance do I give to each? You may want the perspective of Jacques' clients, who may be guests on the boat. After all, entertaining is an important aspect of Jacques' business approach. How comfortable were Jacques' children on the boat? How important is their input? Although there is no definitive answer, your thought process may elicit other possibilities.

An approach that both entrepreneurs and executives in large Fortune 100 corporations take to ensure a breadth of perspective is to establish advisory or corporate boards (known as governance structures) for obtaining important input from stakeholders with various interests. (I'll discuss this in greater detail later in the chapter.)

## Attend to Details

As evidenced by the example of Jordan and Jacques, satisfying customers requires finding out about their worlds and tailoring your offerings to their needs. You read about the importance of finding vital information in Chapter 5. Continue discovering information as you *test and revise* your business strategy by identifying recent changes in your customer profile and patterns of purchasing. Are customers following new trends or shifting their interests? Notice how your business solution addresses customer desires. Although you may already know some customers well, this is not the time to be complacent. Conduct research about your customers and prospects and store this information in your brain for ready access. You'll be pleasantly surprised when you retrieve it easily later. Stored information is not dormant and whether you are aware of it or not, your brain acts upon it as relevant situations emerge. This in turn, will alert you to your relevant internal company processes and systems that can enhance your customers' experiences.

For example, like Melanie and GreenSoap, you may want to fine-tune your payment processes because you need your customers to perceive you as at least as efficient as their bank, travel, and credit companies are in processing requests. Your customers expect and feel entitled to these services. You may refine all your customer interface services to provide that extra amenity—free service, free shipping, warrantees, free loaners, or coffee and Internet access while waiting. Attaining excellence and increasing business are in the details.

## QUESTION IT ALL

"Excellence is in the details" means that when your business is profitable and you think you have the answers, *that* is when you need to *test and revise*. It makes sense to:

- *Dig deep*
- *Dig deeper*
- *Avoid minutiae overload*

Let's look at the example of Skeeter Footwear, with $80 million in company revenues. The company increased sales by 7 percent in two consecutive years and increased operating margins by 1.5 percent due to supply chain enhancements and retail price increases *without* an increase in market share. It was important to find out why

## Dig Deep

Sean Meyer, CEO of Skeeter, deliberated about the significant increase in sales and continued to *test and revise* his business model. "I knew market share wouldn't increase, but I should validate my thinking about this and review the numbers," he thought. As a condition of continuing business with Skeeter, a high-end retailer asked Sean to stop offering his footwear at discount stores. As suspected, the loss of market share in these distribution channels had a strong impact nationwide. Sean decided to monitor revenues and market share carefully in the next several quarters to determine if he made a wise business decision in exiting these channels.

By contrast, Sean's new pricing strategy of raising the price of every pair of shoes by $2.00 across the board, regardless of current price, paid off in significantly increased revenues. This strategy increased operating margins. Skeeter also enjoyed 12 percent combined return on investments and assets. As you can see, market share is not always correlated with profits.

## Dig Deeper

Sean tracked costs and profits for stores in each region by product and demographic. He projected future costs with several what-if scenarios, designing contingency plans for each.

During a review with the team, Skeeter's marketing manager, Frank, observed that new customers yielded a higher profit margin than did existing customers. This surprised the team and the interesting insight created excitement and raised many questions about the product line. One suggestion was to hire an innovation expert for ideas to increase profits with existing customers. Skeeter embraces a culture of change and improvement, and to *test and revise* is an exhilarating process, a way to challenge the business to reach its greatest potential.

### Avoid Minutiae Overload

The Skeeter Footwear team remained focused on profitability. Another company might lose concentration, wasting valuable time and resources on tangential issues such as price points and sales revenues. Of course, Skeeter had its share of distractions, but everyone knew its singular goal was profitable growth, making even the occasional tangent relevant as a possible solution.

Excessive attention to detail can be distracting. The large home goods retailer that did not dig deep enough into the numbers for its small electrical appliances category was distracted by its search for inexpensive real estate. The management team focused on real estate minutiae and lost sight of its strategic intent to upgrade and refresh older stores. Discovering acceptable property values and rents, along with the desire to have a presence close to competitor stores, provided a rationale for these decisions. Year-end results for new stores were good, although not great, as compared with same-store sales of those more than one year old, which were lower than one year ago. One can surmise that the older stores did not receive renovations and upgrades needed for a fresh, vibrant look. When preoccupied and focused on interesting but irrelevant minutiae, the company lost its way and profits suffered.

Was this a strategic move? Did the company learn from these experiences? Although your strategic intent is your road map, it is not a document carved in granite.

### REASSESS YOUR STRATEGY

*Test and Revise* is an ideal opportunity to reassess your strategy. Although some companies find the process too laborious and time-consuming, successful Fortune 100 companies use this iterative evaluation process to discover new paths to greater profits. *Test and Revise* is a best practice built into the standard operating procedures of the most successful companies.

Now is a good time to reconsider your three key questions once again:

1. *What do I want to accomplish?*
2. *What is the current state of my business?*
3. *What is required for my company to become more profitable?*

As you review your previous responses, challenge and clarify your assumptions. Revisit your competitors' advantages. Reassess your product line and business practices.

During a *Test and Revise* exercise, Charlie Gorden of Gorden Steelworks found one of his products eroding into a commodity. When he reviewed results for the previous seven quarters, it told him a story and he acted upon it. Over time, he sold off the remaining inventory, started a consulting division, and focused on producing higher-priced, customized products that his customers were willing to pay for.

Mo (Chapter 6, *Flexibility*) redesigned his PackPlus pharmaceutical packaging after learning about a new trend from his distributor. His own intuition, a colleague's suggestion, and sluggish sales provided the momentum to make the change quickly.

When Kinney Shoes could no longer compete due to competitor Payless ShoeSource's superior operational efficiencies, it sold off its assets and went out of business.

The Internet division of well-respected bricks-and-mortar Babies "R" Us decided to pay UPS Next Day Air for all customer shipments, attaining an advantage over its competitors.

Many superstores changed the traditional operational paradigm by adopting a warehouse model. This changed the landscape of mass retailing very quickly.

Do you have the right customer segments? Can you sell product adjacencies easily? Do you sell by industry or by geography? While most banks sold geographically, Citibank was the first to sell by industry, utilizing a relationship manager model.

Combustion Engineering changed from a product focus to a market focus when Occupational Safety and Health Administration (OSHA) regulations changed, knowing its previous model would be obsolete within a short time. Did this take intense time and effort? It surely did.

Tira Boutique employees (Chapter 4, *Reality*) started sharing suggestions among stores on weekly conference calls. The CEO did not want to invest in exchanging merchandise among the stores, yet agreed that collaboration could result in higher profits. She was correct.

Maybe you do not want to expand your company. Daleen Peters, owner of Miller Carpets, assessed her growing business. She admitted that she did not want greater responsibility and sold her most profitable and growing designer carpet line to a competitor for a very large profit.

It is important to be truthful with yourself during *Test and Revise* before you spin out of control like Douglas and Martin, co-owners of a children's clothing accessories company. Following passage of the North American Free Trade Agreement, the manufacturers bought two plants in Brazil without doing proper due diligence. Their unfamiliarity with local law and customs added so many unexpected costs that the expansion crippled the business and eventually resulted in its demise. Without a plan to *test and revise*, they merely hoped things would get better. After three years, it did not.

In summary, you need to question your methods with an eye toward making revisions by taking these action steps:

- *Challenge your plan*
- *Design contingencies*

The most effective way to *test and revise* is to imagine other scenarios that can influence how you run your business in the future. Anything is possible in the uncertain world we live in.

## Challenge Your Plan

Recall Peekaboo Child (Chapter 7, *Integration*), the $75 million manufacturer of an industry-leading five-piece baby stroller.

Eavesdropping at a Peekaboo Child *Test and Revise* meeting in Wisconsin, you can observe animated conversation and enthusiastic participation by all attendees. One employee makes an impassioned plea for adding adjacencies to position Peeka-boo for growth. Another staff member argues that collaboration, one of the team's metrics, needs a more substantial rating in the performance review process. The topic shifts abruptly when an account manager recounts frantic calls from his largest client who is frequently out of the best-selling $950 stroller. Trudy jumps in, suggesting six instead of five geographic sales and distribution regions as a partial response to the resupply problem.

Similar to Skeeter Footwear, Peekaboo Child focuses on profitability; and like Skeeter, it remains profitable. Although the *Test and Revise* meeting sounds chaotic and even rude at times, those attending view it differently. On a company survey, employees and customers referred to Peekaboo as "passionate" and a "class act."

Peekaboo co-CEOs Josh Evans and Cynthia Whiteman encouraged company banter and challenge from the start of the six-year-old business. They expect their employees to challenge strategic assumptions and company goals, and to plan for contingencies.

## Design Contingencies

Josh and Cynthia support their employees to continuously *test and revise* Peekaboo's strategy and plans. Even in a company run as tightly as Peekaboo, scope creep can find its way into the current strategy and threaten its success. Forums similar to that of a high school debate are scheduled a few times a year to review key questions. Employees hash out arguments for and against each point and create contingencies for various circumstances. Samples of questions are:

- Is our strategy logically defined based on the current market and competition? (*The team defines market and competition.*)
  → How will it change in the next year? Three years?

- → What market and demographic shifts do we expect to occur in the industry? (*The team defines the industry and the demographic segments.*)
- → Does the current positioning make sense?
- Are current operational processes realistic?
  - → Who are our suppliers and what do they need from us? What do we need from them? Who else do they sell to? Are there any conflicts of interest? How can we strengthen these relationships? Do we want to include them in our sales and development meetings?
  - → Are there other suppliers in adjacent markets that we should consider as partners?
  - → Do we have sufficient capacity to keep pace with sales if we make changes to our strategy by adding new products?
- How well is our sales process working? Is the team configured correctly? Do we need to make changes next year?
  - → Are we providing correct and sufficient training?
  - → Who is our competition? How do they sell?
- Does our pipeline include innovations in design and materials?
  - → Are we speaking with relevant suppliers to keep abreast of new technology?

## CONTINUE TO REVIEW

As you continue to review your strategy, challenge your ability to execute your goals effectively. *Test and Revise* can become one of your business's most important practices. Some actions to take are:

- *Agree throughout the company*
- *Implement consultative dialogues*
- *Create governance structures*

When Jim, the new Vice President of Human Resources at Baldwin MediaWorks (Chapter 5, *Obtain Vital Information*), reviewed the company's goals, he found a lack of congruence between many of the goals and the overall strategy. Knowing the importance of agreement throughout the company on such critical issues, he met with the CEO to resolve this issue.

## Agree Throughout the Company

When Jim met with the CEO, Marvin McMillian they decided to clarify the company goals for every employee. To do this, they facilitated focus groups with Baldwin MediaWorks' 125 employees over the course of six weeks to articulate, gain agreement and align the company goals with specific measures. The focus groups also created employee incentive and motivation because of the value placed on their involvement and input. Both Marvin and Jim understood that it takes the focus of all employees working on the most important priorities to achieve results.

## Implement Consultative Dialogues

Many times in this discussion, I have mentioned a variety of review meetings. Because of the importance of providing forums for *Test and Revise*, the *Consultative Dialogue* tool, an essential company lever, is the subject of Chapter 12. You will learn to adopt this best practice throughout your business using examples of different dialogues for diverse purposes.

## Create Governance Structures

As acknowledged earlier in this chapter, advisory and corporate boards can offer a wealth of knowledge about your industry, competitors, customers, and other stakeholders. They provide an outside perspective to balance your point of view.

Advisory boards, which are more flexible and less formal than corporate boards of directors, can contribute ideas and solutions you may not consider from your vantage point as a company owner. Some of these ideas and solutions include product design, new thinking about technology, supply chain management, CEO succession criteria, compensation policies, monitoring criteria including the Sarbanes-Oxley Act of 1992, professional contacts, segmentation, and value propositions, to name a few. Since this topic is beyond the scope of this book, you can find other sources on governance in the bibliography at the end of the book.

## SUMMARY

*Test and Revise* is the PROFITS principle for fine-tuning all facets of your business for profitable growth. Your leadership excellence sets the tone, positions your company for growth, and eliminates the common problem of scope creep.

Leading for excellence is viewing the business from all relevant stakeholder perspectives. It means attending to details. This focus guides a strategic reexamination of your business while avoiding the threat of minutiae overload. As you assess your strategy, use the stories of Skeeter Footwear and Peekaboo Child as examples for how to question prior assumptions, challenge existing mind-sets, test your strategy, and design appropriate contingencies.

As employees continue to review and achieve agreement on company goals, the application of consultative dialogues and the judicious use of governance structures will ensure that *Test and Revise* becomes one of your company's best practices.

## QUESTIONS AND ACTIONS FOR YOUR BUSINESS PROFITS

- Think of a project, current or past, that requires many perspectives.
  - → Who are the important stakeholders? List the information you need from each in order to complete your project successfully.

- Consider your existing methodology for reviewing your business.
  - → In what ways can you categorize the data to provide the best metrics to tell your company's story?
  - → What process do you use to trace your profitability measures back to all your activities?
- What topics typically sidetrack your focus and add scope creep to your strategic intent?
- Design a process to challenge your strategy and design contingencies for possible market changes.

| P | Position Only for Growth |
|---|---|
| R | Reality |
| O | Obtain Vital Information |
| F | Flexibility |
| I | Integration |
| T | Test and Revise |
| S | Steering the Company |

CHAPTER 9

# Steering the Company

*We must cultivate our garden.*

—Voltaire

The PROFITS principles derive from best practices that serve as your road map to sustainable profitability. Your *employees* put the principles into action. Succeeding in your business correlates directly with the initiative, commitment, and caring of the people in your company—and it starts with you.

*Steering the Company* is the effective and efficient interaction of people collaborating in a unified and organized business environment. This principle refers to organizational interpersonal interactions, rather than to individual people.

These interpersonal interactions occur within your company's unique culture, which is deeply rooted in beliefs and values that company employees internalize. It is essential to get your house in order and position yourself properly on the people side of your business because you will be leaving money on the table (your profitability) if you do not. You must pay as much attention to organizational interpersonal interactions as you do to operations, marketing, and sales effectiveness. In this overview, the actions to focus on are:

- *Visualize your company*
- *Be the people leader*
- *Deal with dysfunction*
- *Reduce resistance to innovation*
- *Create a learning organization*

W. L. Gore Associates (Chapter 6, *Flexibility*; Chapter 7, *Integration*) offers an example of an effectively run culture that combines strong norms, interpersonal interactions, and business expectations.

Think of an airplane as a metaphor for your business. A well-oiled engine keeps the plane operating properly. You may need to repair various parts or get a complete tune-up and overhaul. Operating effectively requires a coordinated team—pilot, flight attendants, luggage handlers, ticket checkers, and people on the ground. There are also rules provided by the Federal Aviation Administration (FAA) for safety and appropriate etiquette when flying, including takeoff and landing procedures and the distance between planes. What is the FAA equivalent that operates inside your business? How well does it work?

## VISUALIZE YOUR COMPANY

Find a quiet place where you can relax for 15 minutes. Do not think too much as you go through this meditation. Allow the first image to surface in your mind. Do not argue with it or change it. In fact, you may want to have someone read these questions to you so you can focus without interruption.

Take some deep breaths and begin to let your mind visualize your business. Observe yourself walking through the front door of the building. Are you walking quickly or slowly? What are you wearing? Are you looking straight ahead? If not, follow your gaze and notice what you look at.

Who are the first people you see? How do they look at you? How do feel about them? Does a conversation take place? Is it friendly and relaxed, or is it tense? Is there someone else you speak with before entering your office? What is the first thing you do in your office? Do you make a phone call, check your e-mails, or speak with a colleague?

Now, think about the way you work with people. Do you converse with staff and clients easily? Do you chat about your personal lives or get right into work-related conversations? Are the other people friendly or serious? Do they speak most often of business-related issues? What do they wear—suits, business casual attire, or jeans and T-shirts?

Next, notice how your employees interact. Does your staff gravitate toward those in similar work functions? Do they schmooze and mill around during the day or do they sit seriously at their desks? What is your attitude about how they work? What does their general attitude seem to be?

Are there guidelines for how people behave in the office? Do they answer the phone in a specific way? Do they have morning routines? Do they typically go out to lunch or do they eat at their desks? Do they come into the office and leave at specific hours? Do you have flextime? Does anyone work from home? Do people tend to leave frequently for doctor's appointments and to pick up their children? Do people share their schedules with one another? Do they call each other on their cell phones?

Then, think about your role as leader. How do you influence people in your company? Be truthful—does anyone have a greater influence than you do? How do you demonstrate your leadership? How do you see your strongest beliefs and values operating in your company?

Observe your feelings during this meditation. Is this useful for you or do you think you are wasting time? Are you getting sleepy? Take a few deep breaths to focus. Let us continue now—the meditation will be finished shortly.

Do people in your business have clear roles and responsibilities? How many people are in each functional area? Do employees have specific accountabilities? How does your company communicate these? How do reporting relationships work? How closely do you manage people? How often do managers and their direct reports meet to discuss projects? Do people work most often on project teams or individually?

Does your company have a training department? Are there development plans for each person? How do you select people for executive positions? When there are position openings, do current employees generally move into them or do you hire outsiders? Do you ask people you know in your industry for candidate recommendations and referrals? Do you employ recruiters or use the Internet for hiring?

Do you believe your organizational culture is working? Name three things you would like to change in your company culture. Can you implement these now? What has to happen first?

On a scale from 1 (weak) to 10 (strong), how do you rate interpersonal interactions in your company? What key areas need improvement?

Now, take another few deep breaths. Look around your company again and notice people working. Do you see anything you did not see when you began this meditation? Acknowledge that you and your people work very hard.

Continue to breathe and sense your body seated in your chair. When you are ready, slowly open your eyes, stand up, and stretch.

This exercise offered you the opportunity to reflect on the way people work in your company. As the leader, you can responsibly influence your company's environment and the interactions that occur.

## BE THE PEOPLE LEADER

People are a unique organizational resource that differ from your other capital investments. For one thing, they interact with one another. During the meditation, you thought about how your people interact during their workday. What can you do to ensure a healthy company?

- *Earn respect*
- *Clarify your role*
- *Continue to grow*
- *Stop enabling dysfunction*

There is a saying, "You cannot lead unless people know you care." Your people want to know that you care about their well-being and respect the energy and effort they invest in their jobs each day. When they believe, they will allow you to lead.

### Earn Respect

At a senior team off-site retreat for a 500-employee business unit of a large global corporation, the managing director, Gerard, wanted to include a meaningful exercise to pull his people together and have some fun. Although he did not say so explicitly, Gerard wanted the team to become a cohesive unit that worked together more closely. Currently they each did their own thing.

During the retreat, the team explored both individual and collective strengths and disclosed their areas for improvement. They worked hard developing team norms and guidelines for operating. The team discovered shared interests like sports and hobbies and learned about one another's spouses and hometowns. For example, Diego told Mike, "I didn't know you played soccer or that your wife was from Idaho." By the time they boarded planes for different parts of the world, strangers had become colleagues and friends. Within a few months the business unit more than tripled revenues by collaborating on several projects. Gerard's credibility soared and he acknowledged, "It is so much easier to speak to my team and develop new business now."

## Clarify Your Role

As the entrepreneur of a profitable business, you are held in high regard in many circles. You have credibility and influence you may not even realize. You choose competent team members who accomplish company goals. Could you do better? Most of us can, particularly when it comes to articulating our goals and communicating accountability for those goals.

As the leader of your business, your role is to create a collaborative and amicable culture in which you provide access to what your people need to get their jobs done. Whether yours is a traditional hierarchy, open structure, matrix organization, or some combination of all three, you decide what culture works best, given your vision and how to make it real. If it works, your company will be profitable.

Some large corporations design their culture to be more like smaller companies. For example, Bill Gore of W. L. Gore Associates knew exactly how he wanted his company to operate. "Get big by staying small" was one of his axioms. He wanted people to work closely and collaborate and he found the people to make his vision a reality. With no titles and by means of small cross-functional team projects, W. L. Gore Associates continues to achieve unrivaled success.

The first question the interviewer asked at my initial job interview at Bloomberg L.P. was how to design and adapt the "best practice" talent management systems of large successful corporations without changing Bloomberg's culture. During my tenure, I learned that a small, growing, and profitable company could value systematic processes and remain integrated without changing the open, fast-moving culture at the firm. Most people at Bloomberg, as at W. L. Gore Associates, do not have titles or private offices. People are equally accessible at all levels, and the system works.

Imagine your leadership role if you ran a Fortune 100 company. You would leverage what you do best and find other people to do the rest. You would select people well and delegate responsibility. You would be sure to get the information you need from reliable sources. You would be approachable.

As the leader, you need to find out what is going on without becoming fixated on details. If you do not communicate well, find someone who can articulate your goals to the rest of the company.

Take the time to determine what your limitations are and challenge yourself to answer these questions:

- How much independence can I allow others?
- Am I someone who trusts people?
- How accessible am I willing to be?
- How well do I articulate goals?
- How much money am I willing to provide for assessing and developing employees?
- Do I want to create an internal training division or have people attend courses outside the company?

In actuality, it does not matter how you answer as long as you create an organization that matches your leadership style. Then, if you remain consistent and communicate well, the rest will follow. When you are congruent in your practices, you find yourself hiring people who *complement* your strengths rather than hiring only people who are like you.

The following questions, which should be answered "yes" or "no," will reveal much about your company.

- Do people keep their attention on key issues and establish priorities?
- Are people unfocused and/or scattered in their daily work?
- Do important company processes and systems lead to consistently high performance in cost and operational efficiency most of the time?
- Do company processes and systems aid innovation and creative solutions? Does this company compare well with other companies in this regard?

- Is internal competition for turf as critical as external competition with other companies?
- Is there a sense of urgency in responding to problems and reaching goals?

Now, go back over the questions and ask why you answered as you did.

## Continue to Grow

Learning is exciting for most of us. Can you recall a time when you learned something new about a competitor? Can you remember how the information resulted in fresh insights about your business and your industry? As you research new projects, can you feel your brain clicking away as it pieces bits of information together?

When you find new information about your company or yourself, it is exhilarating—a chance to improve, excel, and grow. Whether you learn by taking courses, reading, speaking with a professional, or watching a television program, your curious mind keeps you alert and open to discovering innovative solutions.

A good example of curiosity breeding success is Henry Ford, who grew professionally and personally by using his intuition and strong relationships. He devised an ingenious solution at Ford Motor Company to foster employee loyalty and sell record numbers of automobiles.

In 1914, Henry Ford lowered prices and increased employee wages to $5.00 per hour during a worldwide depression, when other automobile companies were paying their workers half as much. Why did he do it? He reasoned that higher wages meant more people could afford to buy automobiles. Extra income made every worker a potential Ford buyer. More customers meant lower car prices, for more and more people. More people wanted to work for Ford Motor Company because of the higher wages and Mr. Ford's apparent concern for his employees' standard of living.

How do you cultivate relationships that raise the standard of living for *your* employees, which ultimately helps you and your business? And what are some negative practices you can avoid?

### Stop Enabling Dysfunction

There are habits you can avoid or eliminate in your efforts to become a more effective leader. An important Fortune 100 best practice is to discourage micromanagement and encourage people to become problem solvers instead of complainers. When you coddle or fix employee mistakes, you dampen independent thinking and prevent people from learning. By demonstrating healthy behaviors to employees, such as learning from mistakes and moving forward, keeping sight of goals, avoiding analysis paralysis, and not enabling dysfunction, you model positive behaviors.

## DEAL WITH DYSFUNCTION

Did you ever notice that people pull together and surpass expectations when a crisis occurs? You read about how Mike and Peggy Sarak coped with disaster (Chapter 4, *Reality*) following Hurricane Katrina and the destruction of their restaurant. Why is it that when life is status quo, people do not feel the same sense of urgency to achieve? How can you inject urgency into your present business?

- *Recognize the signs*
- *Cope with change*

Robert Lucky, CEO of Lucky Paints, received a phone call late one Tuesday afternoon in April. "We need enough paint for a 25,000-square-foot office building," said the customer, Frank Robbins, "and we need it by Friday at noon." Taken aback, Robert asked for more information and heard himself negotiate a premium price and then agree to supply the paint.

When he hung up the phone, Robert considered how to position this project to the irascible company supervisor, who was already struggling to keep up with demand. "Hal," said Robert, "have I got a challenge for you." Within an hour, Robert and Hal mobilized plant employees for a 60-hour manufacturing marathon. Hal reluctantly promised to do his best to complete the job. Robert was amazed when he walked into the plant 12 hours later and observed energized hourly workers working swiftly as a coordinated team to fulfill the order on time. Motivated by the challenge, they delivered all the paint within three hours of the deadline.

What accounted for this shift in attitude and effort? Psychologists have long known that dysfunction can zap the full capacity of any organization. In the absence of crippling dysfunction, anything is possible!

Many times, making decisions is a problem during a project. How did Robert and Hal avoid decision dysfunction in this project? The Lucky Paints CEO made dysfunction a non-issue because of his own negotiation of project terms with Frank Robbins. The short deadline eliminated possible conflicts. Lengthy approval processes and authority issues were not obstacles since Hal was the supervisor in charge. Hal and Robert collaborated about measures of success (paint for 25,000 square feet), information, planning, and accountability. Employee attitude was not a problem, possibly because everyone had to be focused strongly on the urgency of completing the project. Therefore, most of the stress of new project decision making reached resolution before the employees began the project.

### Recognize the Signs

Psychologists say that dysfunctional behaviors are more interesting and variable than healthy ones. Healthy behaviors are finite and predictable, but dysfunction is not. As with families, organizational dysfunction is sometimes chaotic and impulsive.

The following are some of the more obvious examples of organizational dysfunction.

You may recognize these in your company. Once the culture of your company adopts these patterns, they are difficult to eliminate.

### Difficulty with Reality

Some people find it difficult and painful to face reality (Chapter 4, *Reality*). Feelings of shame, the belief that a particular reality is too difficult to cope with, and the need to save face lead some people to distort facts. This attitude toward reality can actually become a cultural norm. Sometimes people believe their work is excellent when it is not. Poorly performing managers may believe they manage well and have team loyalty. Others believe that nothing needs to change and that new, innovative solutions will only reduce quality. Thomas Hewitt of Tucker Airparts (Chapter 1, *Achieving a Profitable Business*) believed that things would get better if he simply waited.

### Difficulty with Time

Meetings should be productive and collaborative. More often, they become reflexive weekly or daily habits that distract and waste time. Lack of focus, boredom, and dependence on comfortable routines may be symptomatic of a time management training issue—or they could be indicative of something more insidious that permeates your company. Frequently we stop questioning the usefulness of our meetings and tasks.

What time wasters distract your employees from meaningful work? Leading the long list of offenders are coffee, food, and cigarette breaks. Others include personal Web surfing, schmoozing, too much e-mail, and too many instant messages. How many people in your company say they work best under stress and seem to create anxiety that actually detracts from work? How many times do we fool ourselves and say we will work at home in the evening to make up for wasted time at work and find that we carry our briefcase full of the same work home day after day and never get to it? Many times the frantic race against the clock stimulates high adrenalin levels that interfere with our focus and the ability to think clearly.

### Concern about What Others Think

Think back to the meditation exercise at the beginning of the chapter. How do your colleagues respond when you arrive at the office? How do you act toward them?

In some cultures, employees behave differently when the boss is present in contrast to when he or she is not. For example, they might stay late when the boss stays late, asking to help out but then failing to complete the extra work by the agreed time. They may eat lunch in the office instead of taking a break to deceptively demonstrate loyalty and hard work.

Conversely, a manager might discourage subordinates from meeting with their boss alone, a practice that clearly hinders a culture of openness within the company.

### Generalized Anxiety

Some company environments are constantly fraught with anxiety and peculiar behaviors. People in these organizations are perpetually fearful of losing their jobs. They look for negative telltale signs in every comment by their managers and they are the ones constantly switching from activity to activity without completing anything substantial. Some people talk compulsively or ask questions and may feel threatened when asked to attend a one-on-one meeting. They do not listen carefully to information because they are anxious about what others may say or ask them to do. Others may find it difficult to accept criticism and feedback, never commit to anything in writing, make excuses about their performance, do not respect deadlines, or make conditional commitments based on the availability of other people, the equipment, the economy, the customer, or any other circumstances they can rationalize. By accepting these tactics, the organizational norm is to accept excuses instead of results and the company fails to meet its potential.

When these dysfunctions become the norm, it signifies a critical level of discomfort that can ruin a business.

## Cope with Change

To help people cope with change, maintain your conviction to generate trust and maintain a healthful and positive culture. After all, you put your heart and soul into this company. Now is the time to prove your commitment to yourself that you can persevere through the hard times.

Begin to build trust by speaking more candidly to your employees. If there is a problem, admit it and solicit their input for repairing the damage. You will not be telling your employees something they do not already know and being honest with them makes you more human and approachable. Be willing to take the blame for much of the conflict and confusion, including the times when you looked the other way instead of confronting the issues and the times when you were an equal participant in ignoring reality. Be humble and ask for help.

Many companies begin this trust-building process by recognizing and showing appreciation for their employees, such as Henry Ford's decision to raise wages above those of his competitors. You also read about the oral surgeon who treats his staff and their spouses to a Broadway show and dinner during the winter holidays (Chapter 6, *Flexibility*). Disney's management team inspires trust by aspiring to excellence—for customers in theme parks and for employees in their training. L. L. Bean acknowledges employee accomplishments by giving generous bonuses tied to sales. You probably know other examples.

Another important component in raising company trust and morale is keeping the lines of communication open. Look at your company communication process and ask yourself:

- How do people transmit information? Do they use informal channels or transmit information through the management team? The most effective communication occurs flexibly through many channels. An active grapevine, assuming it promotes work solutions and camaraderie, can be a healthy information mechanism.
- Do you communicate and reinforce your vision throughout the company? If not, who does? If the answer is

no one, then find the breakdown. Determine the best ways to communicate company information. Some companies distribute newsletters while others conduct town hall meetings. What is the appropriate channel for your company?

It is very important to find the 'bad apples' in your company. Troublemakers foment the discontent that lives just beneath the radar. When you identify such people, you may want to give them the benefit of the doubt, that perhaps they are unaware of their toxic behavior or need training to do their jobs more effectively. That said, find out who the problem employees are and provide a strong warning by letting them know that their current behaviors are inappropriate and are not acceptable. If the behaviors persist, take quick action and terminate their employment. This serves as an example for others and demonstrates that you are serious about reform.

For example, a group of employees at one particular company started an intranet chat room for complaining about senior managers, naming them and providing inappropriate information about their families. The CEO immediately intervened. When the same people created a new site under a different name, five people lost their jobs. That was the end of the online complaints, at least on the company intranet.

Some dysfunctional behavior is situational and occurs when the company experiences change. However, there are ways to reduce the resistance.

## REDUCE RESISTANCE TO INNOVATION

As you become familiar with some typical behaviors that occur when your employees resist change, you can find ways to support your employees and sustain a healthy company environment. Innovation is particularly difficult for many people because it challenges familiar ways of doing their work. Therefore, as the company leader you need to:

- *Recognize resistance*

- *Support people*
- *Model a healthy company*

## Recognize Resistance

Renowned social psychologist Kurt Lewin conceptualized what happens during the change process. He referred to the unfreezing process when a person begins to give up old behaviors and add new ones.

People may fear what is happening and feel insecure about what will happen next. The future may seem bleak and threatening. Some people focus too much on pain and rewards. Some employees will feel that the change is marvelous and others will not see anything good in what is happening. For some others it is all too much, too hard, too soon, and too long.

Resistant behavior based on underlying erroneous assumptions about current and future reality can undermine your business. Employees may believe they have to save face when told to do something, and you may see an assertion of autonomy in some people with responses like, "I'll decide what I'll do." Others may protest for the sake of protesting and feel it is fun to say no. Still other people may imitate self-assurance and say, "I belong to the right side and must show it." Still others may be caught in the web of a dare. No one dares back down in an argument.

Learning to identify and understand these reactions against change can help you accelerate the change effort. For example, you can provide a face-saving method by encouraging colleagues to help make the decision in an effort to preserve their autonomy. When people exhibit frustration with a new or threatening task, you can help them to work systematically with smaller parts of the task.

## Support People

Offering direct assistance, engaging people in conversation, providing reality checks, and generating activities to assure small successes are ways to support and encourage people through innovation and change. Rewarding and emphasizing positive attitudes reduces resistance. Soliciting employee input and utilizing their solutions builds trust and promotes greater employee involvement. Recognizing achievements publicly and granting greater responsibility can also work well. Consistent and frequent communication of company goals encourages and supports greater team cooperation in most businesses.

For example, Lockheed, the defense company, supported its employees by offering diversity workshops for every employee at all levels of the company. These workshops addressed ways to deal with employee interactions within the company by helping people understand differences in the way people may communicate depending on gender, sex, race, and multicultural influences. PepsiCo supported stressed employees in the mid-1990s by implementing stress management workshops and the Federal Deposit Insurance Corporation (FDIC) is currently supporting older employees with technical training, as graduating MBA students are joining what has been perceived as an "old civil service" organization. Supporting your people goes a long way in establishing their loyalty and productive contributions.

## Model a Healthy Company

You know your company is healthy when employees view change as routine and not as a crisis. At this point, your colleagues welcome challenges and feel energized by them. The intellectual juices begin to flow and people start brainstorming possibilities and solutions. There is little or no complaining about new projects, and employees remain focused on profitability. People listen to one another and readily approach you, suggesting their own company benchmarks. A healthy company is the solid foundation of your business, and instilling organizational learning is an excellent way to reinforce it.

## CREATE A LEARNING ORGANIZATION

For most companies, three key elements reinforce open communication and create healthy environments for sharing ideas, debriefing projects, and strengthening capabilities.

- *Dialogue*
- *Training*
- *Development opportunities*

Learning is anything that produces new and sustainable results—new ideas, solutions, methodologies, knowledge, and ways to work with others. Within a culture of open dialogue, people ask questions that cultivate learning.

### Dialogue

Dialogue is an exchange of information. In businesses with open communication and dialogue, employees have the opportunity to express their points of view and offer solutions for solving problems and exploiting opportunities. Leaders of companies that encourage dialogue at all levels of the business are models for positive interactions in employee communications with each other. These companies tend to be highly energizing and stimulating. Dialogues can occur anywhere—within small groups, between individuals, in the cafeteria, or in the hallways.

### Training

The knowledge your colleagues require may or may not reside within the company. You can offer company training or create an alliance with other organizations for sharing training opportunities and expenses. You can encourage employees to attend workshops, conventions, classes or to explore networking opportunities at local professional forums.

Although many people think of training as time spent in a classroom, training refers to anything that expands thinking. The best training (and the current trend for education) takes place via online computer learning, within cross-functional teams, town hall type discussion forums, and focus groups. Many CEOs schedule breakfast meetings with a few employees each week. These meetings are similar to fireside chats and encourage informal discussion and collegiality without regard to employee position.

There is greater awareness among entrepreneurs and executives in Fortune 100 companies that best practices encourage internal development of employees for future promotions. Chapter 11, *People Processes*, offers extensive information and methodologies for you to learn and adopt this essential best practice.

## Development Opportunities

Though you can hire a specific skill set from outside your company, in most cases the most valuable information is the knowledge that resides *within* the company. It takes time to learn a company's unique history, culture, and operating methods. Your company is different from any other company, and your employees know how you want the company to operate. When you stay true to your vision and style, employees will want to remain because they are comfortable with the way you run the business.

You have a good idea about who is productive and who supports your vision. You will learn to assess this and then provide your people with appropriate opportunities for greater responsibility. In *People Processes* (Chapter 11), you will learn to develop and retain both your high potential and high performing employees. These are the employees to develop and retain for future leadership positions as you strive towards greater profitability.

Part II of the book demonstrates how to use the seven PROFITS principles in your own company. The next step is learning the *Business Reality Change Model*. This model requires you to use all seven PROFITS principles to assess and solve any problems and explore any opportunities that challenge your business.

## SUMMARY

The principle *Steering the Company* aids you in learning effective, efficient, and healthy interpersonal interactions for your company. *Steering the Company* refers to your people organization, rather than to individual people. The intent is to provide an overview for creating a healthy organizational environment by illustrating how to ensure healthy interactions between and among employees and management.

We began with an exercise to help you visualize how the people side of your company operates. You gained insight into the leader that you are and learned how to earn respect, continue to grow and stop enabling dysfunctional behaviors.

Since dysfunctional behavior is toxic, we focused on recognizing the signs of this behavior and learning to cope with change. Many times change is due to innovation that disrupts familiar routines. To reduce resistance, we first must identify it and support people as we build a healthy company. A healthy company is a learning organization, which includes dialogue, training, and development of leaders and employees.

In Part II, we explore the specific tools for adopting the best practices of the PROFITS principles.

## QUESTIONS AND ACTIONS FOR YOUR BUSINESS PROFITS

- As you experienced the visualization exercise, what did you see in your company or in yourself as a leader that you want to change?
    - → Write down three things you want to change within the next month.
    - → Create an action plan for changing specific behaviors.
    - → Share this plan with someone trustworthy, and meet weekly to discuss your progress.
- What attitudes can you identify in your company when you discuss new initiatives? For instance, are people excited, reluctant, eager, uninterested?

→ List three ways you can influence change effectively.

→ Create a small team that will commit to making these three changes happen.

- How can you create learning opportunities for your employees?

  → Commit to three new forums for employee learning opportunities within the next three months.

  → Communicate your intentions to create more learning opportunities to your employees within the next few days.

# Run Your Business Like a Fortune 100—The Tools

Congratulations! Now that you've reached Part II, it's time to collect your reward. Just as it took you a lot of time to work through the seven PROFITS principles, it took months for me to transcribe my thoughts on paper, because I reviewed my business, too, as I wrote—answering the same questions I posed to you. Frankly, it was difficult to answer some of the questions myself!

We all must confront these serious questions, especially when anticipating how to deal with the unpredictability of global markets. New competition seems to appear out of thin air. It is much too difficult and a waste of time to focus on only one or two competitors when the world is so large and uncertain. Our competition is the whole world.

Many entrepreneurs try to encompass more of the world for their business than is realistic. A few times a month, I receive calls from people outside the United States looking to partner and form alliances. Most are strangers. Currently I have five global partners, two of whom I have never met in person. Our roles are sometimes amorphous, since work shifts from project to project, yet the points of business integration during each project are well defined.

The complexity within any industry is astounding. Enveloped in uncertainty, the only true way to gain and keep competitive advantage is to thoroughly know your customers and design your business processes and systems with the best principles and tools you can to position your company to meet their needs.

Large corporations pay big dollars to design their strategies. The real secret of the most profitable Fortune 100 companies is not only the design of their strategy, it's in how they painstakingly create the linkages that integrate their entire business. That is what I offer you in *Run Your Business Like a Fortune 100*. The key message of the book is to focus on the continuous testing, revising, and integrating that will advance your business to the next level for little or no cost. Linkage and integration are the keys to successful implementation of your strategy, leading directly to profits.

In Part II you learn to work the seven principles of PROFITS into a system of well-running, moving parts. Do you recall the childhood toy with several moving colored gears on a board? When you turned the handle at the edge of the board, all the gears moved in unison. Some gears were small and some were large. None were the same size or color. I remember the exhilaration of seeing all the gears engage and rotate at the same time. This is what I hope for your business!

Here's a preview of Part II.

Chapter 10 introduces the *Business Reality Change Model*, a systematic, structured, sequenced yet flexible approach for evaluating business opportunities and resolving problems. This will challenge you to raise the bar for your company's performance. You will also see it applied to a $20 million business in the automotive parts industry.

Chapter 11 takes the mystique out of complicated Fortune 100 best practices in *People Processes*. I explain how to simplify the complexities of succession planning, leadership development, employee competency designs, performance management, and retaining talent. In the area of talent management, small and medium-sized businesses can succeed in ways that are more difficult for larger enterprises.

Chapter 12 offers the tactical activities for continuous prosperity by keeping your company well linked and integrated with a variety of *Consultative Dialogues*, which include performance evaluations, weekly team dialogues, talent reviews, quarterly business reviews, and best seller dialogues. Equipped with these tools, you will always have vital information for your company within your grasp and ready to help you boost profits!

# CHAPTER 10

# Business Reality Change Model

*A problem is a chance for you to do your best.*

—Duke Ellington

The *Business Reality Change Model* provides the structure to organize what you know (and do not know) to help you decide what to do and how to do it.

You will most likely relate to the company and team I'll use to introduce the Business Reality Change Model. Though you may be familiar with some parts of this model, my team formulated this design for a Fortune 500 corporation. Senior executives throughout every function of the organization used it faithfully—at first because it was required and later because it worked. Although the model works for any company, the application here is to a smaller business, Star Auto Parts, because in my experience small and medium-sized companies have a tendency to jump right in without thoroughly assessing challenges. Why? This is because entrepreneurs are action-oriented and smaller companies have fewer people available to provide different perspectives on the many possibilities most companies need to evaluate.

## INTRODUCING STAR AUTO PARTS

Tim Arthford, CEO of Star Auto Parts, may be in a different industry from yours, but his challenges reflect current market trends for companies of all sizes in any industry.

Star Auto Parts is a private company with annual sales of almost $20 million. The corporation employs 60 workers in its plants in California, Idaho, and Michigan. Tim's senior management team includes two sales managers and a marketing executive.

Star buys used small trucks and service vehicles, which the company refurbishes and resells. It also breaks down vehicles for parts resales. Many of its competitors purchase vehicles or parts from Star for their own customers. The business serves two core market segments: used equipment and refurbished parts. Each segment includes both dealership and competitor sales.

From 2001 to its biggest year ever in 2007, Star Auto Parts' profitability increased dramatically. Then, in 2008, market share suddenly flattened for the whole business and profits fell precipitously.

Until 2008, the refurbished parts segment was more profitable, with market share and sales increasing by 10 percent or more annually. Although sales increased from $18 million to $20 million in 2008, market share failed to keep pace, and actually declined by 0.1 percent. Resales to competitors, previously the less profitable segment, enjoyed an increase in market share but with *no* increase in sales.

Tim puzzled over the situation and decided that his best course of action was to focus on increasing market share in Star's historically most profitable line—reselling parts and vehicles directly to end customers—while deemphasizing sales to competitors.

Ask yourself now: What should Tim do next? With widely different options available, each likely to result in different consequences and operational requirements, Tim needs a reliable method for evaluating Star Auto Parts' most profitable solution.

## Why Might Tim and Star Auto Parts Be Important to You?

To some degree, all businesses face similar competitive pressures. The pace of change is too fast and the choices too numerous to allow you time to think about what you need to do *right now*, let alone predict what you will need to do in the next six months to a year. So where do you start? How do you take the general principles of PROFITS and use them to evaluate your options and take action?

## THINKING ABOUT PROBLEMS/OPPORTUNITIES

While we may know what we want to accomplish, we generally use past and current performance as our guide, disregarding or not even realizing what we need to know before starting the evaluation. For most businesses, applying the PROFITS principles will provide the background against which current and future work will take place. The seven principles also give you a way to *link* where you are now to what you are trying to accomplish.

Let's say you've decided you want to increase profitability by 10 percent in 2010. How does this decision *position you for growth*? What does it mean for your current product lines and your output capacity? How will it affect products already in the development pipeline? Is this target *realistic*? Will realizing this increase in profit margin offer you the *flexibility* required to adapt to a changing market?

These questions may be daunting, so let's simplify the challenge with an example. Say you want to begin work by 8:00 AM. You start by thinking about the internal and external factors between you and achievement of your goal. It seems simple, but now think about all the factors involved. There are external

**179**

threats or opportunities beyond your control, such as the weather or changes in your children's or your spouse's schedules. And what about your own strengths and weaknesses in controlling your own behavior? Once you consider these and many other factors, you know exactly what limits your ability to begin work by 8:00 AM. At a minimum, this knowledge may motivate you to make changes that help move you directly to your goal.

Your assumptions about internal and external factors influence how your company may respond when anticipating opportunities and solving problems. These in turn affect how the Business Reality Change Model can work for your particular situation. The model uses a sequenced approach to assessing business opportunities and resolving problems systematically. It works best when put in the hands of a small team whose members have authority and accountability and who challenge one another to raise the bar for your company's performance.

## KEY ASSUMPTIONS AND CONTEXT FOR THE MODEL

Let's begin with some of the key assumptions entrepreneurs may have about their companies. Notice your reaction as you read these.

### It's Easier for a Small or Medium-Sized Company to Change Quickly than it Is for a Large Corporation

People cite the collegial, friendly climate of smaller companies, where innovative changes happen quickly and easily. In fact, many small business owners left large companies precisely because of politics and bureaucracy that get in the way. Here are some of the issues that large corporations face when attempting even small changes:

- Cumbersome structures, silos, and lack of integration.
- Inherent sluggishness in decision making, approvals, and purchasing.

- Inadequate financial controls.
- Redundant processes and too much functional overlap.
- Shallow leadership pool.
- Lack of cross-functional knowledge.
- Poor communication exacerbated by too many layers and silos.
- Lack of accountability or awareness of who's accountable for what.
- Misalignment of measures among departments.
- Lack of clarity about assumptions.
- Unclear corporate objectives.
- Uneven knowledge and understanding of corporate goals from layer to layer in the organization.
- Tendency to focus too many resources on internal issues rather than customers.
- Misalignment of key work processes.
- No coordination among mission-critical information technology (IT), management information systems (MIS) and financial control systems.
- Weaknesses in some parts of the company that lower the efficiency and effectiveness of the entire company.
- Lack of focus and prioritization—a "ready, fire, aim" culture.
- Sales disconnected from other functions.
- Over-ordering and excess inventory created by vendors' volume discounting.
- Complacency that sets in when success blinds the organization to the risk of commoditization by competitors that replicate what the company does.

Jim Kravitts was senior vice president of a large consumer goods company before becoming CEO of ShiptheContainer. Asked about his tenure in the large organization, he is quick to opine: "You just couldn't get anything done there with all the layers of people involved in making even simple decisions." He knows exactly how he wants his current company to stay different: "I don't want to become bigger. We make changes quickly. The funny thing is, I actually use many of what are considered best practices in large corporations. But now I can make things happen quickly that took months to implement in the big company. Go figure."

Many entrepreneurs like Jim Kravitts have learned to break large company best practices down to their essences in order to integrate change faster, build in *flexibility*, operate with minimal bureaucracy and become more profitable than their bigger competitors.

### There is No Such Thing as a Small Change

All changes spark a chain of events that affect everything around them and set off a cascade of new ones. Everything builds on everything that happened before. Fortunately, you have a nearly omniscient perspective that allows you to understand patterns, connect the dots and acquire a thorough, cohesive, and authentic point of view.

### You Need to Balance Stability and Change to Avoid Unnecessary Chaos

In *Steering the Company* (Chapter 9) you read about the importance of establishing equilibrium between tasks and people. Too much change can throw this balance into chaos. To establish stability, you must choose appropriate people to work on change issues. Cross-functional teams generally work best because the variety of perspectives generally results in better decisions. People with differing points of view educate each other about the implications of any modifications and the team's breadth of experience will reinforce an equivalent breadth of the vision. Knowing the culture, norms and values of your company, including the ways people solve problems, make decisions, deal with conflict and interact on teams, will guide you toward a sustainable equilibrium between stability and change that employees can accept.

As you focus on the future, you will also find the balance between stability and change. Your tolerance for ambiguity will become more apparent and you will make better choices about which risks are worth taking.

When redefining relationships with customers and employees during times of change, you can fine-tune the stability-change equation if you see an overemphasis toward either the tired past or the uncertain future.

### Accept That Your People May Have Difficulty Moving Beyond an Internal Focus

As with the large corporations, your company may also tend to focus on an internal point of view. Why? This internal focus is simply an easier perspective to maintain. You control your own processes and can impose changes. By contrast, the marketplace and your customers are unpredictable. Focusing on what is unknown and uncharted will exhaust you long before it produces positive results. However, concentrating on current and prospective customers instead of yourself is a prerequisite to success. You need to avoid the tendency to keep fixing and streamlining internal processes and systems to 'get ready', *if* they are already at or close to efficiency.

### People Overestimate the Capabilities of Their Own Company

Entrepreneurs tend to overestimate their company's core capabilities and their employees' ability to stay realistic (Chapter 4, *Reality*). While confidence is good, arrogance will get you in trouble. It is important to stay disciplined, learn from mistakes and remain humble, particularly when the market is unpredictable—which is *all the time*. In layman's terms, be sure to keep your ego in check.

### Challenges and Goals are Like Dynamic, Living Organisms

The world is constantly changing and the plans you make today may not be relevant in a few weeks or months. You need a

**183**

structured course of action to move your business forward. *Test and revise* your assumptions and plans as you acquire new information. Each time you test and revise, new patterns and insights may surface. By frequently correcting course and avoiding wishful thinking and its illusions, you are far more likely to achieve your goals. The bottom line: Everything has to fit right, both outside and inside. Maintaining realism and focus ensures your profitable growth.

### Learning is Continuous

The most successful and knowledgeable entrepreneurs tend to be receptive to the ideas of other successful and wise people. As you advance in your business, cultivate bonds with people you respect—those who can help you evaluate your ideas. Colleagues with experience in areas where you are deficient can offer needed perspective as you grapple with difficult decisions. Being receptive means you are almost always open to continuous learning and observing changing customer and industry patterns. Circumstances change quickly and your ability to learn, accept change, and adapt rapidly is what keeps your business sustainable. Now let's get to the model!

### BUSINESS REALITY CHANGE MODEL

The Business Reality Change Model consists of three essential phases that underscore the critical thinking required for excelling at problem solving and decision making. Although you may be familiar with the ideas comprising the model, it is unique in its emphasis on linking the parts.

The phases are:

- *Problem/opportunity question*
- *Detailed assessment of external and internal reality*
- *Summary and next steps*

Here are the details for each phase, followed by a real-world application to the situation faced by Star Auto Parts and its CEO.

## Problem/Opportunity Question

A problem/opportunity question asks about a core business issue. When addressed, it solves, preempts or anticipates a critical situation. The question initiates an intensive analysis of your market, customers and company. If it is ambiguous or incorrectly focused, this problem/opportunity question will not be relevant and/or actionable.

Here are examples of problem/opportunity questions:

- How can we increase market share in the X product line?
- How can we enter the X market?

## Frame of Reference

One of the most important and frequently overlooked features of a problem statement is the frame of reference. The frame of reference is essential to provide boundaries for your analysis. Is your frame of reference a particular market, industry, location, or product? What is your time frame for achieving your solution? The frame of reference focuses your entire business analysis by providing important parameters for your assessment.

## Business Analysis

This is the heart of the process. You already have a solid problem statement with a frame of reference that is focused, yet broad enough to include all relevant information.

The first step of the analysis is to gather both external and internal *vital information*. It is best to gather the external information first since it provides insights that may affect your internal analysis. You then need to transform this information into usable knowledge for solving the problem. Because this process is iterative, you will *test and revise* the information often to make sure it links to your problem statement and frame of reference. Linkage is critical.

Typically, the best way to obtain *vital information* is to ask and answer *who, what, where, when, how,* and *why*. At the end of your questioning, you will know the most important information for each category. If you are not able to answer all the relevant questions, then you lack important data. Getting in the habit of asking and answering these questions—by reading and attending industry conferences and forums—will systematize this strategic focus.

### External Analysis

Start with significant information about things beyond your direct control, such as the environment for your industry and business, the competition, customers, and end users (the customers' customers).

Other industry and environment information includes size of market, targeted segments, current and future trends, growth, relevant historical influences on present circumstances, and legal and government considerations. It may also include demographic changes and trends in financial markets, along with global, industry, cyclical and profitability considerations.

What do you know about your competition? Who are they? Where do they compete? Are there new entrants to the industry you have not considered? What are your competitors' strengths and weaknesses? How do these competitors respond to change? What do they do differently than you and their other competitors? Do they provide the same services for your customers as you do?

Who are your customers? Why do they need your product or service? What else do they buy? What is important in their lives, and how does it affect their relationship with you? Think about other customers in the chain, especially those who may buy from your customers. How well do you understand what motivates them? What do trends indicate about potential new customers?

These are only suggestions, and you may have others to add. The main point is to address thoroughly all issues that matter to you. Go beyond skimming the surface. Remember that the analysis requires you to obtain and use only data relevant to your frame of reference.

*Following a comprehensive analysis of each category, create a summary statement of the most important findings that emphasize the most relevant information for addressing your problem statement and frame of reference.*

## Internal Analysis

Now let's turn to the effectiveness and efficiency of your own systems. Internal processes and systems include operations, human resources (policies, compensation, training, development, recruitment, selection, succession planning), logistics (distribution and transportation systems), product development and product building, financial systems, marketing (promotions, advertising), and sales. What are your systems' strengths and weaknesses? How effective are your processes and systems in helping you complete tasks on time and within budget? Do they help you accomplish specific goals?

Frame of reference is very important to consider here too. Do you have available financial liquidity and working capital? What are your constraints? What is your debt-to-equity ratio? How do your financial ratios interrelate? What does it cost to produce each product? How do material and labor costs affect the value chain? What are the opportunity costs of various projects, including your breakeven analysis, payback period and net present value? How do these things affect your profitability over the duration of your frame of reference? What combinations of financial measures (such as performance against goals to increase margins, inventory turnover, or cash by lowering operational costs) affect your profits?

As you think through cross-functional considerations, how do operations, sales, marketing, human resources, technology, research, and development interact with one another?

When you think about operations, consider plant locations, machinery, distribution, production capacity, warehousing, materials, purchasing, logistics, packaging and other relevant value chain components.

Marketing analysis includes demographics, segmentation, brand management, pricing, advertising and public relations, media, promotions, and market research.

Technology may include engineering, database and computer software, as well as the capacity to innovate.

The human resources department is accountable for organizational structure and culture including how people work together individually and in teams. This consists of assessments of capability and talent, employee census and company policies.

Relevant sales analysis includes information about your sales organization, including size of sales force, strength of customer relationships, expectations of the sales force, sales training, forecasting, and selling patterns across your frame of reference.

### Summarizing the Analysis

You are probably familiar with the SWOT analysis, which uses the familiar 2×2 matrix to chart your internal strengths and weaknesses and your external opportunities and threats. It is critical that you take your SWOT information directly from the external and internal analyses and that all the data links directly to your problem statement. The Business Reality Change Model derives its power from the connections among its components. It is also useful to do a SWOT analysis for each of your key competitors. You may be surprised at how little you know about them, which highlights your vulnerability.

At the conclusion of the SWOT analysis, you then summarize the key takeaways: Limitations, Horsepower and Sustainable Competitive Advantage.

**Limitations** resulting from threats and weaknesses *must be addressed*. Once recognized, you need strategies and plans to remedy them.

**Horsepower** includes those strengths and opportunities that help build the business. Once you identify these, you will leverage them to solve your problem or determine how to maximize the opportunity you choose.

**Sustainable Competitive Advantage** is something unique to your company that provides the basis for long-term profitability. This is your primary lever for influence.

## BUSINESS REALITY CHANGE MODEL ANALYSIS OF STAR AUTO PARTS

Here is the analysis for Star Auto Parts, discussed earlier in the chapter. It follows the steps illustrated above.

### Problem/Opportunity Question

Initially Tim Arthford, CEO, decided to work on the following problem:

> How can Star Auto Parts increase market share in its most profitable line?

### Frame of Reference

Tim reviewed his data and noticed something interesting. Although prevalent across the board, the decline in market share was most serious in one location—Detroit, Michigan. He reasoned that the problem needed correction within the next six months if his company were to maintain its current profit level. This was because the market environment changed rapidly within the past year and Star Auto Parts already lost significant market share.

Based on his research, Tim focused his problem statement even more precisely:

> How can Star Auto Parts increase market share from 7 percent to 10 percent in its most profitable line, in Michigan, within six months?

### Business Analysis

Include all you can think of that is relevant for your problem/opportunity and frame of reference in your external and internal analysis. At the end, you will summarize with your key takeaways/findings.

#### External Analysis

In examining market conditions, Tim learned that the weakening U.S. dollar was dramatically changing the availability of raw materials and the prices of products that Star Auto Parts requires. This downturn—specifically the decline of the housing market and resulting decrease in home renovations—was responsible for a decline in customers who use small trucks and vehicles for their work in construction-related building and service industries. Steel prices were going up, resulting in higher prices for new and reconditioned parts. As a result, many small auto parts companies were going out of business, leaving fewer players in the market. With its 25-year history, Star Auto Parts is a major competitor in the industry.

However, Tim also discovered that the weakening U.S. dollar discourages people from buying new vehicles. Historically, many small truck owners replaced their vehicles when the warranties expired. Now they were likely to keep them and replace worn parts. In that sense, this $6 billion parts industry remained strong. Interestingly, many vehicle sellers were finding it more profitable to sell vehicles for their scrap steel value, which was then selling at a premium. People also sell their used vehicles overseas, and the weak U.S. dollar was causing parts dealers overseas to import more scrap steel. Competitors of Star Auto Parts have overseas customers who want to buy both parts and scrap.

A new web site for used vehicles and parts simplifies the buying and selling process between competitive sources. There are 750 people in the trade who pay a monthly fee of $1,200 to participate in the web site program and compete only on price. Star Auto Parts stands by its quality, preparation and packaging, which gives it a competitive advantage. However, only someone who has experience with Star Auto Parts knows of this advantage.

Star Auto Parts' inventory is variable and dependent on customers. Inventory can be large at any time and prices vary depending on market sensitivity and the product's time on the shelf. Price flexibility is arbitrary.

*In summary, due to the economic downturn, many competitors are out of business. Many customers have also gone out of business, particularly in the building trades, due to the mortgage fiasco and a poor economy. Steel and scrap prices are high. People are either holding on to their vehicles longer or selling them for scrap, often to overseas buyers. A trade web site simplifies this price-based trading. The high monthly fee creates a barrier to entry for many other competitors, an advantage for its 750 international members.*

*Star Auto Parts has a strong 25-year history and positive reputation. Inventory is variable based on customer need.*

### Internal Analysis

Star Auto Parts has no outstanding debt, $5 million in inventory, a $750 million line of credit, $500,000 cash and a 95,000-square-foot warehouse in Michigan. Last year Star Auto earned a $1.25 million profit.

Despite this solid foundation, Tim believes there is room for improvement in his marketing, sales, human resources, and pricing competencies. Customer turnover was high in the past three years, due primarily to high volume of Internet purchasing.

Star Auto Parts has very low employee turnover. One of the production employees provides technical training. Sales commissions are based on sales, not profits. This is significant since profitability is decreasing. Pricing is variable, and salespeople provide flexible pricing for customers with few guidelines and little consistency. Until now Star Auto Parts decided not to compete with low price competitors on the Internet. They followed the same policy for purchasing. When a customer requests a product, the purchasing department obtains the product without regard for price.

Production standards at Star Auto Parts are industry-based with plants operating on two shifts. The Michigan plant, the one in the frame of reference, operates with zero defects and excellent efficiency.

Tim believes there is an opportunity to market Star Auto Parts more effectively. Customer relationships can be stronger. There is little advertising or promotional activity in trade journals or presence at professional organizations.

*In summary, Star Auto Parts has the financial resources to improve marketing by emphasizing and building customer relationships. A new sales compensation system could focus on providing incentives to increase profitability and reverse the decline in market share in the core business, by selling directly to customers and dealerships. Star Auto Parts can also compete on price for Internet sales.*

## Summarizing the Analysis

Remember, the problem question for Star Auto Parts is:

> How can Star Auto Parts increase market share from 7 percent to 10 percent in its most profitable line, in Michigan, within six months?

Tim's SWOT analysis uncovered the following:

- *Strengths*. Star Auto Parts has a 25-year history signified by quality relationships by those who know the company and a solid reputation, a feel for the business, good quality, loyal employees, a strong operational supply chain, and available liquidity.
- *Weaknesses*. The sales force model rewards revenue over profitability, the best product line is currently the least profitable, inventory sales are variable and there is a lack of integration with customers.
- *Opportunities*. These include: fewer players in the market than there once were, relationship building with customers, dealers, and online competitors, people repairing instead of buying new vehicles, resellers wanting more scrap for overseas customers and buying whole vehicles, integration of dealers and large customer databases.
- *Threats*. The poor economy means fewer customers for small trucks due to businesses dissolving, the U.S. dollar is decreasing in value and steel costs are increasing, competition is based on price—there is little loyalty.

As Tim examined the key SWOT points, he reviewed all the information in his analyses thus far. Finally, he summarized all the data into Limitations, Horsepower and Sustainable Competitive Advantage.

### Limitations

Star Auto Parts must be willing to compete on price with concern for the competition, especially online for reselling parts.

### Horsepower

For Star Auto Parts, horsepower includes a 25-year reputation for quality and loyalty from those who know the company. Other areas of horsepower to build quickly, certainly within the six-month time frame, are stronger relationships with dealers and competitors both online and offline, including integrating Star's database with those of its dealers. The company can also change the sales compensation system immediately to reward profitability on the key product line yet continue to reward Internet sales based on revenue generation, since it is already doing very well.

### Sustainable Competitive Advantage

Star Auto Parts can leverage its reputation and history in the business by focusing on building strong relationships with customers continuously, whether this is face-to-face sales, integrated databases or competitive pricing for repeat business. A strong sales compensation system rewarding profits rather than only revenue generation positions Star Auto Parts for the future.

## SUMMARY

This introduction to the Business Reality Change Model provides the *critical thinking phases* of a powerful tool for analyzing your business. It utilizes the seven principles of PROFITS in a comprehensive, easy-to-use Business Reality Change Model.

As you become proficient with the model, you can build on it to create specific plans and activities to execute the solution to your business problem or opportunity. These will fall into place easily and you will be confident that you are working on the correct issues and have the *vital information* you need to create and execute your next steps.

The most important part of the model is the linkage among the phases. The problem/opportunity question and frame of reference directly set the boundaries for the external and internal analysis. Be sure not to extend the scope of the analysis, because though it may be interesting, you will get bogged down and lose sight of what is most relevant to your problem/opportunity question.

The key phases are:

- *Problem/opportunity question*
- *Detailed assessment of external and internal reality*
- *Summary and next steps*

Following these phases of the model, you will be able to create action plans that include accountabilities, measures and monitoring of key milestones.

## QUESTIONS AND ACTIONS FOR YOUR BUSINESS PROFITS

- Utilizing a key challenge for your business, write a problem/opportunity question.
  - → Review this question with several trusted advisers.
  - → Apply each phase of the Business Reality Change Model.
  - → As you do your analysis, utilize PROFITS principles in your thinking.
- Teach the Business Reality Change Model to a colleague in another company. This is the best way to make sure you understand it.
  - → Suggest that your colleague use the model for a business challenge.
  - → Critique each other's work and suggest enhancements for the best thinking.

# CHAPTER 11

# People Processes

*Learning is not attained by chance, it must be sought for with ardor and attended to with diligence.*

—Abigail Adams

You may think that because you are an entrepreneur with a small or medium-sized company, systematized people processes are not relevant to you. But in fact, you will learn in this chapter that the way you think about and organize your staff's performance and development is among your most important business decisions.

There is a leadership drought in many companies across the globe. Only one-third of Fortune 500 CEOs remain in a company for more than three years. Even more alarming, one-third of companies on the Fortune 500 list in 1975 *no longer exist*. In addition, most merger and acquisition failures are the result of a leadership gap and the lack of cultural integration between the merged companies.

We live in a world of chaotic and constant change. Many companies focus only on short-term results to satisfy impatient shareholders. Companies tend to act quickly to exploit cost reductions and short-term revenue growth that actually destroy rather than create value. Many of these companies fail to spend the time or money required to recruit or develop talent, sacrificing long-term financial benefits for short-term gain.

It is a leader's job to assess the long-term consequences of actions like those mentioned. You want to lead a company that produces excellent results, and to do so, excellence must pervade everything you do. When your people execute their responsibilities with excellence, then your company builds a reputation for quality and reliability. Excellent people work harder and take pride in their work. According to internationally known psychologist and author Dan Goleman, top performers exceed revenue targets by 15 to 20 percent more than average performers.

Leadership begins at the top of company—in the CEO's office with you. You set the tone and expectations with your behavior and values. Even though developing talent is identified as a key competency for leaders, it receives the lowest rank in attention in formal leadership development programs and action taken by managers.

In a research study by Corporate University Xchange (Leadership 2012), 97 percent of companies studied said they have concerns about the bench strength of their current leadership. Top management in these companies also said they did not have the ability to develop leadership talent to support the company's future growth objectives.

**The critical issue is that leadership is in short supply.**

You have probably seen or heard the term *war on talent*. More than a dramatic analogy of doom and gloom, this increasing shortage of talent in companies is a serious global threat. It is particularly problematic within the United States for the future of our long-term economy.

How does this war play out? The converging forces of aging workers and retiring baby boomers, tech-savvy Gen Xers and Gen Yers venturing into the workforce, and the general shortage of skilled workers will result in an approximate

15 percent decline in the U.S. talent pool by 2015. This is especially true for those in the 35- to 44-year-old range in more traditional companies. Almost two-thirds of senior leaders leave an organization within the first three years of their recruitment into the company. Besides the high hiring and severance costs for these employees, the huge knowledge deficit that remains for an organization—*the loss of practical experience gained through leadership*—is costly. The Employment Policy Foundation reports that by 2030, the United States will experience a labor deficit of 35 million workers.

According to a recent study completed by McKinsey & Company, most companies are ill prepared to win the talent war. Sixty-five percent of company executives believe they lack sufficient talent in their leadership ranks. Search firms are growing twice as fast as gross domestic product (GDP), as companies reach outside their own businesses for management candidates. Although 78 percent of respondents said line managers should be accountable for the quality of their people, only 7 percent believed this was actually happening within their own organizations. Only 10 percent of executives said that their companies retain most of their high performers. Yet *many leaders are unaware of how severe the problem is*—all the way up and down the management line in many companies, not just the Fortune 500. The true impact of employees coming and going in the unintegrated company—with its fragmented functions and projects—is unclear to most managers. They do not know what is happening in many parts of their organization, even as they pay lip service to the problem.

Though some executives think outsourcing to emerging markets is the answer, this move usually elicits mixed results. Talent is hit-or-miss with many overseas positions. These positions typically fill back office functions rather than executive suites. As industrialized nations continue their evolution into service economies, the world is moving in a direction where we place a premium value on talent. The *Economist* reports that intangible assets like the value of leadership have increased in value for companies in the S&P 500 from 20 percent in 1980 to almost 70 percent in 2008.

A fundamental shift is clearly occurring and the average management team's primary responsibility is changing from accessing and managing capital to accessing and managing *talent*. Finding and managing talent is becoming the number one concern of managers in every company. If you look at companies like Google, eBay, Apple, and Microsoft, companies with few hard assets, it is obvious that their true worth is measured by the strength of their intellectual property and people.

As a successful entrepreneur, you are in a position to make sure you are not trailing behind in the war for talent. While your company is still small enough, you can and must address the talent imperatives of your employees before you lose them.

Ironically, the good news for you is that **many Fortune 500 companies will increasingly lose talent to small and medium-sized companies**.

This is an extremely significant development for small and medium-sized businesses. You have the unique opening within your company to provide disgruntled former corporate employees with the opportunity to make excellent contributions when you utilize Fortune 100 best development practices. And, as luck would have it, the development of best leadership practices follows easy-to-do rules and remains fairly consistent over time.

Excellent people do not go to mediocre companies. They go to places where they find challenging work and the chance to develop valuable skills. Excellent employees are lifelong learners. While they are not necessarily the 'most intelligent' people, excellent employees consistently improve their performance by learning and applying new skills.

Companies that take the time to attract, select, engage, retain, measure, and reward their employees' contributions in meaningful ways *always* have a competitive advantage over those that do not. These companies do not simply strive to develop the individual employee; they endeavor to bring the *entire company* to the greatest heights of performance.

We next focus on *how* you can learn and take actions to apply Fortune 100 processes and create a competitive advantage in people assets in your small or medium-sized business. You may be familiar with terms like *talent management* **and** *performance management*, which refer to large and cumbersome Fortune 100 processes that, at their worst, are intimidating and difficult for even large corporations to manage well. In fact, many senior management teams delegate components of performance and talent management to outside consultants who devise even more unwieldy competency models, succession planning models, training and development departments, and measurement programs. Often fragmented and administered poorly, they create more chaos and costs than the problems they attempt to solve.

When designed and implemented as a fully integrated system, people processes influence how employees work. They reinforce the underlying values the CEO and senior management team model, making these values credible and serving to fortify and enhance your business.

As you adopt the best practices of large Fortune 100 companies by simplifying and adapting them to your company, you can assess, develop, and integrate your talent and performance processes.

A small or medium-sized business, because of its size, can quickly gain a competitive advantage by adopting even one or two of these practices—and probably incorporate them faster and better than a larger company. When your competitors begin to grasp that you attract the best talent in the industry, you will already be far ahead of them by the time they attempt to catch up. As you continue reading, you will find out why it will be difficult for other companies to replicate what you do.

## PERFORMANCE MANAGEMENT AND TALENT MANAGEMENT

*Performance management* is the ongoing process of assessment, feedback, and coaching that improves employee performance.

*Talent management* refers to a system for creating and sustaining a competent workforce that is able and ready to achieve your company's goals. Components of talent management include training and development, competencies, leadership, mentoring, coaching, succession planning, high potentials, recruitment, retention and selection.

This discussion of *People Processes* begins with key assumptions that underlie success. You may not agree with all of them or you may have a different perspective. The following premises address some of the misconceptions many people have about performance evaluation and development within their companies and provide the context for the chapter. They also draw on years of my own and my colleagues' experience working in this field.

## KEY ASSUMPTIONS ABOUT PEOPLE PROCESSES

Before you design a people process, it helps to be aware of the most current thinking in the field. More important, think long and hard about what will work within your unique company.

- *All your employees want to contribute their best to your company and learn all they can.*

  If you can remember this about your employees above all else, you and they will be on the right track most of the time. If there is anyone in your company about whom you do not believe this, cut your losses immediately and let them go. You cannot afford the negativity they bring.

- *Leadership and management require different skill sets.*

  You may be CEO of a small company with only a few employees. In that case, you are both leader and manager. However, these are different roles, and it is important to know the difference between them. The leader views the organization from a strategic vantage point—mobilizing employees, keeping them focused, and inspiring them to follow the company vision. The manager is responsible for day-to-day operations of the team including setting goals, organizing the work, delegating, motivating and developing employees in their daily jobs. Certainly, there is overlap between the two. However, a company requires both roles. If you tend to be more comfortable in one or the other role, find someone who can complement your skill set.

- *Prior to developing employees or evaluating their performance, determine the necessary organizational core capabilities.*

  You need to determine what capabilities your business requires to be profitable both now and in the future. Determining these organizational core capabilities *positions you for growth*. The core capabilities also establish the competencies or skills your employees must have to achieve the company's goals. If the core capabilities are inaccurate, everything else will be wrong. Later in this chapter you will learn a quick and easy way to establish these core capabilities.

- *Behaviors mean more than ideas, documents, and conversations.*

  Actions and behaviors lead to results. Thinking and ideas can lead to and shape behavior but are not the same as behavior. When you read *Steering the Company* (Chapter 9), you reflected upon the powerful influence that behavior exerts on business results. As this chapter unfolds and the discussion focuses on development, performance, and outcomes, it becomes apparent that behavior is the critical measure of success.

- *Discussions about development and performance take place at different times.*

  It is important to separate these two processes so employees can focus their attention on each. Performance deals with how employees do their jobs—how they perform. Performance discussions include the assessment of an employee's strengths and areas for improvement. A performance discussion should not take place at the same time as a development discussion. A development discussion focuses on new skills to learn. When employees are in the process of developing new skills or learning a new job, they will initially stumble and make mistakes as they gain competence. Evaluating them at the same time they are learning, only makes it difficult and stressful for learning to occur.

- *Promoting people or giving them more responsibility is more than a new title.*

  Every position requires preparation and skill development. People often become managers because they are excellent individual contributors. However, managers and individual contributors require different skills. The same holds true when people who manage one person or a small group of individual contributors become managers of other managers. The skill set changes, and people need preparation and training to achieve competence and success in their new roles.

- *On-boarding (joining a company) requires intensive assimilation.*

  When you hire someone into your company, the new hire cannot be successful unless someone mentors him or her in the company's cultural expectations. It is unrealistic to expect a new person to learn the job and the culture without assistance. The quicker the individual learns the ropes, the sooner you will reap the benefits of your investment in this new employee.

- *Your company needs both high-potential employees and high-performing employees.*

  Not everyone in your company will be a star or be capable of performing in an executive position. In fact, you do not *want* everyone vying for executive roles. High-performing employees who are excellent in technical roles are the ones who support and boost high-potential employees to their peaks in the company. Be sure to appreciate and retain them.

- *The most successful people in your company may not always be the smartest but are the ones most capable of and interested in learning.*

  Many studies indicate that those who learn well (sometimes referred to as being "learning agile") are the most successful. They grow from their mistakes. They embrace new ideas and learn to generalize solutions to a variety of situations. They may not have the highest cognitive abilities, yet they possess a tremendous amount of perseverance.

- *Though every job and level in your company requires different skill sets, there are such things as screener skills.*

  Screener skills refer to a set of skills that are not specific to a particular job. However, they are necessary skills, attributes and characteristics to working in *your* company and may include things like adequate intelligence and interpersonal skills, action orientation, technical skill, customer-focused orientation, ethics, and honesty. If you hire someone without these screener skills, the individual is not likely to succeed. There are other skills, too, that uniquely supplement your company's core capabilities. However, the aforementioned screener skills are usually the must-haves to invite employees to your door.

- *Training and development are primarily for the company.*

  Along with physical and financial assets, your company has people assets. Certainly, you want to treat people with respect and let them know you value their contributions. However, the money you invest in training and development is for enhancing a capital asset. You may utilize development as a retention tool. You may offer seminars and send people to conventions as a reward. However, do not hold the attitude that you are doing this for *them*. You are doing this to upgrade *your business assets*. This mind-set will help you avoid unnecessary angst and resentment, particularly if people leave.

- *It is easier to leverage strengths than to improve weaknesses.*

Encourage people to use and develop their strengths. This is rewarding and easy for them. Attempting to eliminate weaknesses is a disheartening and constant reminder of inadequacy. The best you can hope for is that people *minimize* their weaknesses. If they refuse or are unable to do that, chances are they will eventually derail. Unfortunately, this happens frequently.

- *Someone who is reluctant to take risks, deal with change or manage uncertainty, no matter how smart and diligent the person is, probably will never be a high-level executive.*

  You will be a great, as well as less frustrated, manager if you accept this fact. The above characteristics are the most difficult to change. A smart, diligent person can be one of your best performers—one who manages the details and keeps your business operating each day. However, these people are not likely to be your next CEO.

- *No matter how young or old you are or your company is—plan for successors.*

  Having a succession-oriented mind-set propels you forward and advances your business to the next level. You will be compelled to think continuously about developing people, repositioning and enhancing jobs and business requirements, and looking toward the future. It drives you to create a pipeline of immense talent.

## PERFORMANCE MANAGEMENT PROCESS

The debate about the merits of employee evaluations tends to be passionate and heated. For most of us, an evaluation is unpleasant because performance management marks the place where individual ability and situational constraints often collide. Perhaps this discomfort is a carryover from the anxiety with which we met our childhood report cards and the ensuing pride or disappointment of our parents. Therefore, for performance management to be effective, managers must treat employees with the utmost respect and sensitivity during the process, no matter how bad the news.

The purpose of performance management is for managers to provide feedback for improving employee performance—for them to perform to the best of their abilities. Companies have many ways of encouraging feedback using a variety of formal and informal venues. The objective here is to provide you with:

- Specific guidance for understanding essential concepts in designing and implementing an effective performance management system.
- Steps for designing and implementing performance management process components.

## GUIDING YOUR THINKING

A performance management system requires a great deal of forethought, research, and input. The related literature abounds with pros and cons of performance appraisals, rating systems, whether or not to abolish evaluations, passionate arguments about undermining intrinsic motivation, and the rigidity of goals and pay-for-performance benefits and liabilities. Key topics that fall under any discussion of performance management include:

- *Measure what matters*
- *Clarify goals and measures*
- *Communicate goals and measures for performance*
- *Use many data points for performance evaluation*

Though the process can be overwhelming, it helps to start by asking two questions:

1. How can my performance management processes support a high-performing culture for competitive advantage?
2. What does my company require to ensure that our performance management processes effectively and meaningfully achieve this goal?

**205**

## Measure What Matters

Although requirements of your stakeholders, customers, employees, and company's profitability are not the same, you can find overlapping priorities among them. You can use this knowledge to set goals and design measures to highlight your achievements. A coherent performance management system aligns your goals and measures with other stakeholders and tells the story about what accomplishments your company values most highly.

## Clarify Goals and Measures

Your analysis should have well-defined characteristics. The acronym SMART will help you remember to keep your goals and measures Specific, Measurable, Actionable, Results-driven, and Tracked with realistic time frames. If you start with your company's major problems and opportunities, as captured in the summary analysis in the *Business Reality Change Model* (Chapter 10), you will find it easy to write and communicate your goals. Be sure to use metrics that address these problems and opportunities directly. Focus on measures that lead directly to profitability. For example, market share or inventory turnover may be appropriate metrics, but only if they result in profits. You may recall that market share alone may not be profitable when prices are low and when market share represents the volume of a commoditized product. You should be able to capture this distinction by choosing your problem or opportunity carefully.

## Communicate Goals and Measures for Performance

Communicating goals and measures is not a one-time exercise. The human condition resists behavioral change even when there is a conscious commitment to the change. Use frequent feedback, supported by rewards and consequences, to stay on track. This takes commitment from both the manager and employee.

A manager's major role is to know the people he or she manages. This includes observing and assessing employee performance. It is a time-intensive and continuous process, and as the company CEO, you need to communicate to your managers that it is time well spent. If your company is small and you do not have managers, or if your managers have major work responsibilities of their own along with managing work through people, your priorities may conflict. If you want your business to operate effectively, managing people must be your main priority. If work performance is poor or inconsistent because people are not clear about what to do and are not receiving feedback about how they are doing, then what is the point of their employment?

## Use Many Data Points for Performance Evaluation

You and your managers should be collecting data continuously. It is the manager's role to document both positive and problematic behaviors in many venues. This observation can take place at meetings and during interactions with other employees, customers, and staff. A variety of data provides a well-rounded and more accurate picture of your employees' performance.

## STEPS IN THE PERFORMANCE MANAGEMENT PROCESS

If you follow these steps *after* you do the appropriate research and preparation, you will have a rudimentary Performance Management Process that you can fine-tune over time.

### Step 1: Determine Core Capabilities

What are the three to five core capabilities that are your company's competitive advantage?

Most Fortune 100 companies spend thousands of dollars figuring this out with consultants. The quick and easy way is to ask your management team. It is as simple as that. When you have a consensus, you have your answer. If you do not have a consensus, hammer it out over several hours until there is agreement among you. Core capabilities may be some of the following: first to market, market adaptive, market quality leader, employer of choice, stakeholder relations, fast decision making, cost leadership, knowledge focused, financial acumen, or any other capability you believe sets you apart as an industry leader.

### Step 2: Establish Leadership Competencies for Success

Many people refer to leadership competencies as the soft skills. Examples of leadership competencies are: establishes and drives vision, change leadership, innovative thinking, pushes the performance envelope, partnership, plans, strategizes, evaluates. Again, most Fortune 100 companies hire consultants to study their organization and determine executives' competencies through an exhaustive interview process. Still others utilize months and sometimes years of time with their own organizational development experts to do the same thing.

Studies show that at the end of the day, most companies have the same or some variation of the same 10 competencies. This proves two things. First, leadership skills do not vary all that much. Although certain situations may require specific proficiencies, the majority of behavioral and attitudinal skills that lead to success are common to most leaders. Second, you do not have to waste time reinventing the wheel. Although one model may refer to "innovative thinker" and another may refer to "thinks out of the box," and still another may refer to "pushes the envelope," you can easily extrapolate that all these labels refer to a person who is receptive to shifting the known paradigms. Right? The point is you *do* want to evaluate people on leadership competencies. You can find lists of successful leadership competencies in hundreds of books. Use them.

### Step 3: Establish Job Competencies for Success

Job competencies, unlike leadership competencies, take time and effort to determine. One choice is to do what the Fortune 100 companies do and what I did several times. This is to conduct extensive interviews within every department for every job. It is a great learning experience and can be fun and interesting. However, I find that what works just as well is to speak at the same time with both the person who does the job and the person to whom the job reports. Ask them to tell you seven accountabilities that the job entails. This is not a job description. This is what people are actually required to do. Once you have these seven accountabilities, describe them in one or two words. Now you have some basic job competencies.

## Step 4: Design Measures

To design the appropriate measures, refer to your list of job and leadership competencies. What metrics define the accountabilities for the seven job competencies? Ask if these measures truly define how a person demonstrates mastery of each competency. The key is to focus on *outcomes*. The question you need to ask is: What is the outcome or result of achieving this competency?

Everyone should be accountable for the same leadership competencies. The only difference is that those employees who manage others will additionally be accountable for management competencies. The measures you design for each level (i.e., individual contributor, manager, senior leader) will vary in terms of the leadership expectations for the position. For example, someone in an entry-level sales position will not have the same level of accountability as a senior sales representative with major accounts.

You will also have to determine criteria for your measures. What is satisfactory performance? What is outstanding performance? What is unacceptable performance? As you become proficient in performance management, you will develop standards, which in the beginning may be overwhelming and frustrating. You must give it time and remember that this process requires frequent fine-tuning. The more you familiarize yourself with the literature on ratings, forced rankings, weighting, and other performance nomenclature, the more comfortable you will be with the process. However, as long as you know your job competencies for success and utilize measures that correspond to success, you are on your way to a good performance management process.

### Step 5: Match Measures to Rewards

Matching measures to rewards engenders lots of controversy and discussion. You will have to decide what makes sense for your particular company. This depends on the values you instill in your culture and the agreements you have with your employees. Some of the choices are to reward individual performance, reward team performance, reward customer interaction differently than leadership, or institute a merit pay program. Each choice has pros and cons. The key is to think through the effects each choice can have within your business.

### Step 6: Create a Schedule for Formal Feedback

Earlier I said that feedback needs to be frequent. Performance management is a process, not an event. Behavioral change requires time and patience. Although most of your feedback will be informal, it is supportive and reassuring to arrange a formal process a few times a year. A formal process becomes a milestone. Ironically, when a milestone approaches, people complete goals.

Establish and communicate a schedule for formal evaluation and feedback. People will appreciate knowing that there are specific times dedicated to assessing their performance. Remember, few people want to evaluate others or be on the receiving end of a performance discussion. By putting a schedule in place, the process becomes palatable. The next chapter, *Consultative Dialogues*, describes the components of a performance review.

## TALENT MANAGEMENT PROCESS

As stated earlier, first evaluate, then develop. Intuitively, it makes sense to put the two processes together, and many companies do bundle them. However, if you think about it, most people associate performance with compensation and rewards. When focused on your future pay and future with the company, too, it is difficult for both you and your manager to have the mind-set to concentrate on development planning.

The key people processes adapted from Fortune 100 company best practices encompass three primary areas:

- *Competency development*
- *Employee/leadership development*
- *Succession planning*

The correct mind-set for a company's management team is always to *position for growth*. In the "Key Assumptions about People Processes" section earlier in this chapter, you read that employee development is principally for the company, not individuals. To build on that, as you *position your company for growth*, think about current needs, with an eye toward the future. You always look at where you are now and then consider where you want to be. In the gap between these two points, development takes place.

## COMPETENCY DEVELOPMENT

You now know how to determine your company's core capabilities, your leadership competencies and your job competencies. This is a good start for thinking about employee development—which should really be leadership development. That is because as you *position for growth*, you want a company of leaders—people who are responsible and accountable for the company's future, whether they manage themselves or manage others. Anyone who does not have a leadership mindset, which means accepting personal responsibility for what happens in the company, is someone you should seriously think about asking to leave.

## EMPLOYEE/LEADERSHIP DEVELOPMENT

Most Fortune 100 companies pride themselves on having a leadership brand—a competitive advantage that positions them as a culture of stars, change agents, game changers, marketers par excellence, or any number of possibilities. Most firms have a burgeoning desire for recognition as people capital magnets, where the best and brightest clamor to work.

Leadership development adds an element of personal satisfaction, motivation, and commitment for most people. The next step in this development process is learning to:

- *Revise, test and link capabilities and competencies*
- *Develop real work opportunities*
- *Recognize derailers*
- *Identify promotion development opportunities*

Performance feedback, a combination of accolades and areas for improvement, can be a humbling experience. Your message is that you see the person's leadership potential and you are spending time and money to bridge the gap between current and future performance.

### Revise, Test, and Link Capabilities and Competencies

Now is the time to *revise and test* your core capabilities and verify their applicability for the future. Depending on your company's and industry's horizon this may be six months, a year, or perhaps longer. Following that, *test and revise* your competencies for this new time frame. These become the new performance indicators for managing your talent pool. And these are the *only* skills you should develop.

### Develop Real Work Opportunities

As with all areas in performance and talent management, how to train and develop people is a huge area of debate. The key is to know what each training venue provides and what you can expect as a result of the training.

Courses are lots of fun and a great source of networking, cross-functional sharing, and knowledge. People have a day or more away from their routine jobs and enjoy an overall refreshing experience. However, it is costly to be away from work. Courses are expensive and the payoff is chancy. Learning how to do something is not the same as doing it. Even with practice sessions, there is a difference between performing in the safe environment of training as compared to performing on the firing line in the job.

Studies demonstrate that learning on the job, as long as the opportunity for knowledge, practice, and debriefing can take place with a mentor or coach, provides the best learning. Real work is motivating. Though you may not be able to afford a coach for every person, there are many other creative ways to manage job learning. People can work with learning buddies. Coaching can occur in groups with the added advantage of input from several perspectives.

Offer challenging assignments to senior managers whom you expect to move to higher levels in your company to prepare them for greater responsibilities. You can offer these assignments as projects prior to moving people into new positions. This provides time for people to learn and for you to observe. Assignments can include cross-functional moves, turnaround situations, responsibility for larger strategic projects, an increased sphere of responsibility, managing greater numbers of people, and other possible learning experiences that you and they may improvise together. Remember to set clear objectives and measure results so you can provide useful feedback. Written development plans provide criteria and document expectations. You can find examples of development plan templates in books and online.

## Recognize Derailers

Sometimes the strengths people have in one job can become their liabilities in another job. We all know people who are confident and then become arrogant, or the fun-loving person who becomes distracting and annoying. Usually feedback and motivation can help people modify these tendencies. However, liabilities can often derail a career. You need to face *reality* about these derailers or your company will suffer. It is difficult to confront people who derail, especially when the person in question is someone you like, who is loyal and produces good work.

Derailers may be people who do not manage others well. They are too hard or too easy on their staff. They may micromanage and not be good at delegating or developing people. They may not be aware of their developmental needs or may present obstacles to another person's ability to move forward, sometimes seeing their direct report as a threat to their own promotability. At other times, people may not want to be leaders or may simply be uninspiring. Others may not walk the talk, may have difficulty managing their work, or do not fit into the company because of a different value system, different pace of work, defensiveness, or poor instincts.

It is critical that you apprise people when you see potential derailers and take steps to manage these issues before they become business liabilities, something that can occur very quickly in a small business.

### Identify Promotion Development Opportunities

Not all management opportunities are the same. A manager who oversees an individual contributor has responsibilities that differ from someone who manages only other managers. Navigating these leadership passages from one level to another requires important development interventions and training. The larger your company, the more you need to pay attention to these variations. Delegation and reliance on others significantly increase as a person manages larger teams of people.

### STEPS IN THE PROCESS FOR LEADERSHIP DEVELOPMENT

There are five steps that when done well, ensure that your company has a competitive advantage in leadership development. This competitive advantage enables you to be more profitable by attracting and retaining talented people.

1. Identify individual strengths and areas to develop.
2. Design opportunities for learning with specific measures that lead to profitable growth for your company.
3. Follow up on development plans at least monthly.
4. Set a timeline for change.
5. Keep the process going.

As employees grow and develop, you may consider them for other positions within your company. The movement of employees into positions of greater responsibility is a component of succession planning.

## SUCCESSION PLANNING

Many people get unnerved when succession planning comes to the forefront, especially in smaller companies. Entrepreneur CEOs say, "I'm not ready to retire. I just started this business a few years ago and we're doing great," or "I am the company. Even though I have employees, I'm the one who gets the business and has the customer relationships."

Successful succession planning management will:

- *Ensure your future*
- *Identify high-potential and high-performer leaders*
- *Track your company's leadership progress*

Though you may believe you are the company's future, the best insurance you have for your company's future profitability is to have talented people in your pipeline.

### Ensure Your Future

By continuously developing leadership skills and a leadership pool throughout the company, you have a high probability of sustaining your success. This is one Fortune 100 best practice that can cause the best trajectory for future growth—no matter the size of your company.

You may want to review the first few pages of this chapter regarding the war on talent. Though your company may have all the important slots filled for now, an uncertain future may require new and different skills and job configurations.

This is why a continuous assessment of core capabilities and competencies, along with future-oriented job and task analysis, is essential.

## Identify High-Potential and High-Performer Leaders

Although there are excellent methods of assessing people on specific skills, many of us know when we see a winner, especially when it is someone we know well and observe frequently.

Companies need both high-potential and high-performing leaders. High-potential leaders are the big picture thinkers. They tend to be strategic, require fresh challenges often, are usually change driven, can deal with company interpersonal issues, and enjoy challenges.

High-potential leaders *need* high-performing leaders. These high-performing leaders are experts, usually with the depth of knowledge in their field for solving tactical, day-to-day issues. They have strong relationships and the respect of people they work with. High-potential leaders taking on a new challenge, which is what a high-potential person enjoys, need high performers to help them assimilate in their new roles.

As an entrepreneur, you may find it difficult to understand that some people enjoy what they do and are not always looking for new opportunities. Yes, they want stimulation and challenge, yet they want these in areas where they have expertise and depth of knowledge.

Both high potentials and high performers are valuable to your company. However, developing a high potential is more difficult because of the breadth and scope of learning and feedback involved. High potentials, as they move up in the company, like you, will manage and lead the organization from a big picture perspective.

Another area of debate in the field is whether to tell someone he or she is a high potential. You may want to observe such people in a few roles before you let them know. This alleviates possible disappointment if things do not work out. However, in my experience, you want both high potentials and high performers to know their value to you and the company. You also want to let them know how you perceive their role in the future of the company. This provides them with the opportunity to share their goals and negotiate their career track. For example, a high performer may want a new challenge in a cross-functional or turnaround project and may surprise you when he demonstrates abilities you did not know he has.

## Track Your Company's Leadership Progress

Generally, it is the person or department responsible for human resources who tracks the people processes. In the most successful Fortune 100 companies, the senior human resources leader is part of the CEO management team, providing critical input for the future leadership and current capabilities within the company.

It is important to have ongoing statistics about the people side of your company.

Keep track of positions you have in each department. If your company is small, it is even more important to keep track of all the skills the people in your company have for the current business and for the future. Carefully analyze the skills necessary for the near future and be sure that you are developing some of your people in those competencies.

Also, track how many people within the company fill new positions or take on new and different company projects. How often do you hire someone from outside because the skills do not exist within? What are your retention rates? How often do you lose people you want to keep? Do you know why they leave—the real reason and not the story they tell you?

Are you evaluating and following up on training and other learning experiences? What feedback are you hearing? What feedback are you using? How well are learning experiences congruent with the strategies, core capabilities, and core competencies for your company's success?

## STEPS IN THE PROCESS FOR SUCCESSION PLANNING

The following are practical best practice steps you can adopt for your succession planning management program. These are basic steps and as you fine-tune them over time, you may lengthen the list.

1. Select key positions within the company for a future talent pool.
   - Redesign these positions if necessary.
   - Clarify competencies/factors for success in these key positions.
2. How should the organization fill key positions?
   - What percentage of vacancies in key positions do you want filled from within the company?
   - What percentage of vacancies in key positions do you want filled from outside the company?
3. When do you need someone ready for this position?
4. If appropriate, select someone within the company to develop for this position.
   - When do you want the person to be ready for the new position?
   - Who will be accountable for this person's development?
   - Determine learning needs for the person in this position.
5. Specify learning objectives for the person.

6. Specify learning resources and strategies to achieve learning.

7. Evaluate learning outcomes.

8. Determine how to keep track of people identified as potential successors in your company.

## SUMMARY

We addressed topics and key issues for performance management and talent management design and implementation. After reviewing current thinking about the war on talent, we looked at key assumptions and perspectives on people processes. For each process, there was a summary of steps in the process.

Regarding Performance Management, you learned some of the main areas to consider:

- *Measure what matters*
- *Clarify goals and measures*
- *Communicate goals/measures for performance*
- *Use many data points for performance evaluation*

You asked two important questions:

1. How can my performance management processes support a high-performing culture for competitive advantage?
2. What does my company require to ensure that our performance management processes effectively and meaningfully achieve this goal?

As you increased knowledge about Talent Management the importance of core capabilities and competencies again took precedence. We then moved to employee and leadership development and focused on:

- *Revise, test and link capabilities and competencies*
- *Develop real work opportunities*

**219**

- *Recognize derailers*
- *Identify promotion development opportunities*

The final process, Succession Planning, highlighted:

- *Ensure your future*
- *Identify high-potential and high-performer leaders*
- *Track your company's leadership progress*

Next, you will learn the importance of *Consultative Dialogue* for gaining the knowledge and creating the social connections that bridge strategy, tactics and healthy functioning as your ongoing best practices.


## QUESTIONS AND ACTIONS FOR YOUR BUSINESS PROFITS

- Review your current performance evaluation process with your management team or advisory group.
  - → Design three improvements for this year.
- Determine the core capabilities for your business today.
- Think about successors for the positions that are responsible for day-to-day operations within your business.
  - → Determine the core competencies (leadership and technical) for these positions.

# CHAPTER 12

# Consultative Dialogue

*Courage is what it takes to stand up and speak; courage is also what it takes to sit down and listen.*

—Winston Churchill

You climb rugged terrain in this book as you navigate the road to sustainable profits. As you continue to zig and zag, what can you do to maintain a company culture that defies market unpredictability and provides continuity and cohesiveness?

Consultative dialogue (CD) is a best practice that serves your company well on its journey to stability and success. Consultative dialogue focuses on the *exchange* of ideas and information within a framework of business goals, rather than the more common one-way communication flows that characterize many meetings. Certain words come with baggage, and *the meeting* tends to be a big offender precisely because of the one-way ineffectiveness it often implies. I have deliberately changed the name of this process to *consultative dialogue* to suggest a difference between the two kinds of interactions. The purpose of consultative dialogue is for attendees to *consult* and *participate actively*. This involves interaction, give-and-take, cooperation and action.

When you nurture an environment that encourages challenge, growth, and camaraderie among people with varied experience and expertise, all can learn from one another and increase their competence. We all spend many hours at our workplace. When the give-and-take is good, it is very good, and when it's bad ... well, it's bad. There are mechanisms you can put in place to ensure that your company personifies a positive and profitable climate. Consultative dialogues enliven the professional environment by challenging people and supporting effective outcomes. Unfortunately, they can also appear to be structurally similar to meetings, which conjures images of long, boring recollections of being held captive by a pontificating boss. The key difference between participation in consultative dialogues and participation in meetings is the way people interact. A consultative dialogue encourages more active listening, more participation from attendees, and less zoning out. It generally delivers a much higher level of engagement as well.

In this overview of best practices for information exchange, you learn how to organize consultative dialogues for maximum results, followed by what happens during a dialogue and outlines of five detailed CD models that can lead to enhanced profits and successful work environments. These dialogues are:

1. Performance
2. Weekly Team
3. Talent Review
4. Quarterly Business Scorecard
5. Best Seller

## ORGANIZING CONSULTATIVE DIALOGUES

The process for organizing successful consultative dialogues takes account of several essential considerations.

### Clarify the Purpose

Before you collaborate to engage in consultative dialogue, circulate an agenda to make sure all understand the purpose for getting together. An agenda helps you manage expectations and avoid surprises during the dialogue. It allows people to think about issues in advance and it clarifies upfront who will attend, what will be discussed and when and where the consultative dialogue will take place. Generally, the person who calls for the dialogue prepares the agenda. However, anyone who knows the purpose, participants, and desired outcome can do this.

### Ask for Input to the Agenda

The more involvement you generate prior to the consultative dialogue, the more likely you are to achieve its goals. Asking for input encourages people to consider the topics in advance. Sometimes asking attendees to read a document or answer a question as prework helps focus their thoughts. The agenda sets the focus and becomes a pre-dialogue for each person as they think about the issues at hand. Instead of providing opinions or information off the top of their heads during the consultative dialogue, they will offer meaningful and thoughtful input. Preparing attendees in advance allows for review and consideration of alternatives.

Busy people, however, do not usually take the time to review an agenda before a meeting. That is why the consultative dialogue needs to earn a reputation in the company for being too important to miss. For example, someone may suggest inviting a valued customer or supplier to share his or her important perceptions and ideas. The net result of asking for advance input is to encourage participants' involvement and interest in the important proposed topic of the consultative dialogue.

## Assign Roles During the Consultative Dialogue

People tend to play different roles within group interactions. Some people come with these roles preassigned, some adopt them by choice and others have roles doled out to them during the meeting. The purpose of assigning responsibilities during the consultative dialogue is to promote an orchestrated flow and to have each position serve as a learning opportunity for participants. Roles are generally determined at the beginning of the CD and eliminated when the dialogue ends. Each CD should have new role assignments that include facilitator, timekeeper, and scribe. The job of facilitator is the most difficult and important. It requires keeping participants focused and on track while adhering to guidelines for the dialogue such as listening and keeping interruptions to a minimum. The facilitator usually does not offer opinions and has responsibility for highlighting and summarizing key points offered by other attendees.

## Bring Only New Information

One company I worked with held a follow-up meeting after the main meeting to decide which points should be told to the senior team. After the meeting with the senior people, there was another debriefing prior to meeting with the CEO. The consultant (whose idea it was to hold the aforementioned meetings) met alone with the CEO to tell him what was coming from his senior team the next day. Not surprisingly, at the formal meeting with the CEO, instead of taking notes, people doodled on their pads while the CEO smiled and nodded at the information he (and everyone else) already heard.

Does this sound familiar? The key takeaways from this story are: Please do not waste your time and everyone else's by creating redundant meetings that rehash information that people already know. Do not use consultative dialogue as a forum when an e-mail or a telephone call is sufficient.

In contrast, another CEO with whom I worked welcomed the chance to hear fresh, new information when he met with his senior global team for monthly updates. With little interaction between meetings, the CEO was eager to hear information about goings-on in each country and division. He would ask probing questions that generated areas for problem solving and discerned further opportunities for business. Though sometimes contentious, these dialogues spawned enthusiasm, creativity and workable solutions quickly. In fact, these exchanges became my inspiration for the consultative dialogue tool.

## THE DIALOGUE

Dialogue is the productive exchange of ideas, opinions and information. If you do not begin a dialogue when you speak with someone, then send an e-mail or a report instead. It is incredibly important to open the lines of communication from a project's beginning. During a consultative dialogue, the attendees listen attentively to grasp what others are saying. They ask questions for clarification and for elaboration. The facilitator directs the flow constructively as he or she focuses on the responses of the participants and the quality of information. This is what makes consultative dialogues so stimulating, serious but also fun. They work best when egos remain outside the door, along with the posturing, domination of the conversation, and the frequent one-upmanship we often observe at traditional meetings.

People quickly learn that CD serves an important purpose; otherwise, they would not be meeting. As a result, they respect each other's time and use the dialogue in a meaningful way. They feel empowered because they know their participation is essential for determining the solutions. And in order to establish an environment that encourages this kind of constructive, collaborative dialogue, it's best to set a few ground rules—and take some preparatory measures.

### Set Guidelines for Behavior

Guidelines such as "listen," "don't interrupt," and "use brevity to make points" become useful prompts during the excitement of the dialogue. The facilitator generally states these reminders and posts a few on a flip chart or whiteboard at the outset. This should take less than five minutes. The key is to reinforce the guidelines during the meeting. Training people on how to use the guidelines (and to participate in these dialogues, for that matter) is also very effective.

### Review Prior Action Items First

Every consultative dialogue ends with action items for the next one, based on what was flagged for resolution and who is accountable. Make sure to review these action items at the start of the next dialogue. This focus on finishing business energizes people and quickly prompts discussion. In the absence of prior dialogues, briefly review the background relevant to the purpose of the current dialogue.

All actions and solutions that emerge during consultative dialogue must ultimately lead to important actions and/or profitable solutions (and can include other important goals such as humanitarian or social consciousness goals); otherwise, it is not necessary to take the action.

That is the very purpose for getting people together and for your business. There will be a chain (that sometimes may seem indirect) that leads from A to B to C to D and then to profitability. Too many times, it is just assumed that there is some reason, albeit undefined, for doing what you are doing. However, it is important to demonstrate and agree on the logic behind all ensuing actions at the meeting.

### Select Viable Alternatives for Solutions

After some initial background discussion of the topic, problem or opportunity, brainstorming begins to elicit a variety of ideas. The purpose of the brainstorming process is to bring out ideas, not to evaluate them. Following the idea generation stage, you should determine assessment criteria that *do* evaluate the ideas. Ultimately, the participants select the most viable alternatives for problem solving and compare them against even more realistic and practical criteria until a direction and/or solution emerges.

You must do more than merely select the most popular suggestion. This process should build the best possible outcome by taking the most favorable parts of some or even all of the ideas and building a plan that incorporates the most effective aspects of each of them. Not only will this yield a better idea, it will be a collaborative method of solving a problem. It also makes implementation and ultimate success much more realistic since *each person* and his or her idea has a stake in the success of the final plan.

### Solve It Later

As a rule, there will be many more issues raised during productive dialogues than may be immediately addressed. Agree at the outset that only the most pressing issues must be resolved during the dialogue. Occasionally, solutions are apparent and easily agreed upon. Most issues, however, require the brainstorming that results in a few viable alternatives. At this point, it works well to assemble a task team to determine solutions within a realistic time frame. The issue becomes an agenda item for a follow-up consultative dialogue for input and closure.

### Observe the Interaction

Although the majority of us are not body language experts, we can all tell when something exciting is happening. We know when we feel stimulated and when conversation is flowing easily. We can observe when people pay attention or when their minds drift. Watch people's responses during the consultative dialogue for clues to how they are engaging. Pay attention to the animation on people's faces. Look for gestures that signal emotional connection with the topic and speakers. Attend to both

**227**

the quantity and the quality of participation, to both speaking and listening. Emotion can raise participation and intensity of the dialogue. Voices rise, interruptions occur, and when properly handled by the facilitator, participants recognize that the consultative dialogue is working.

## Summarize and Document

The summary of a consultative dialogue contains only this important information: key issues, decisions, actions, account-abilities, and results. One person should be assigned as note taker and another as the summarizer of the meeting. The summarizer is person who provides and collects feedback sheets, synthesizes them, and sums up people's observations and thoughts. The summary is distributed to CD attendees, and may also be appropriate for those who did not attend.

## CONSULTATIVE DIALOGUE MODELS

Equipped with the knowledge of what consultative dialogue is, what it looks like, and its purpose, you can now look at the five spheres where CD contributes most effectively to your business.

## Performance Consultative Dialogue

The earlier discussion of the Performance Consultative Dialogue in the *Performance Management* section of the previous chapter, continues here. Always remember that this dialogue is an interactive meeting between *two adults*—never a humiliating confrontation akin to a parent-child interaction, (which unfortunately takes place in many company performance reviews). Those involved in this dialogue must prepare ahead of time. The person who has requested the dialogue should propose and create an agenda.

Make sure that no one is blindsided during the dialogue. Preparation should include feedback about relevant and specific behaviors. Generalities do not help people understand or change what they are doing. The focus is on accountability, expected results, and next steps. As mentioned in the previous chapter, performance dialogues should be frequent, ongoing and comprised of a few formal interactions a year.

## Weekly Team Consultative Dialogue

A weekly team consultative dialogue is just that—an ongoing way to keep the entire team abreast of fast-changing events. Everyone stays in the loop, hears information, and is in the same place at the same time, which promotes immediate action and decision making. In many Fortune 100 companies, global participation is routine with technological assistance. Given the advances in video and audio technology, people do not need to be in the same room. Whatever the venue for participation, with all CDs you will want to send an agenda to participants before-hand. You may also choose to invite customers and suppliers periodically to provide input.

Stay on track regarding key issues during the dialogue. Focus on the impact of these issues, clarifying desired improvements, actions, and expected results. Create or assign accountability for plans and responsibilities. You may be familiar with the weekly meetings that retail giant Wal-Mart's management team has. These dialogues inspire creativity and participation and result in continuous improvements and long-term profitability. With my own teams, conducting weekly team consultative dialogues heightens motivation and leads to an orientation toward problem solving and taking action.

## Talent Review Consultative Dialogue

Talent reviews are consultative dialogues attended by senior management for reviewing company talent. They serve as a forum for brainstorming about internal and external recruiting and for speaking about the highly charged process of terminations. The dialogue focuses on current company needs and expected changes in the future. You want to address development and training issues for those employees you view as future leaders and decide how to invest in these activities. The company's size determines the time allotted and the participants invited.

## Quarterly Business Scorecard Consultative Dialogue

This dialogue is an opportunity to *test and revise* the Business Reality Change Model. By reviewing your problem/opportunity question, objectives, strategies, core capabilities, plans, measures, and time lines, your company will focus on its most important priorities. You may want to conduct separate dialogues to concentrate on strategic issues and operational issues. Typically, most traditional review meetings highlight the operational side of the business, which tends to be easier to discuss since performance data is readily available.

A strategic dialogue may focus on short- and long-range issues raised by operational reports and include items like longer-term strategic implications for committing to a customer focus and what this means. Strategic dialogues are usually broader in scope than operational dialogues and may cover trends and modifications in objectives and goals. Operational dialogues pertain to monitoring performance against plans or the results on revenues of short-term actions. These operationally focused dialogues may address issues regarding the supply chain, such as logistics, on-time delivery, vendor compliance and so on. During these dialogues, the management team takes the opportunity to review what is going well, what needs changing, what to keep doing and what to stop doing.

## Best Seller Consultative Dialogue

These *reality* dialogues give attention to the company's best-selling products and/or services, helping businesses compare targeted projections to actual performance. Many Fortune 100 companies begin their week with a Monday morning dialogue. This dialogue is usually concise: 30 to 45 minutes is generally enough. Some examples of questions for the agenda are: What are the top three sellers? What are the lowest sellers? How long should we keep the low sellers? Can we come up creative alternatives for marketing our products better? What can we do to increase revenues? Are the margins adequate? How can we increase velocity? Which customer segments are most profitable? Do we observe shifting trends? Did we learn anything new about competitors?

## SUMMARY

Your role as an entrepreneur of a profitable business demands an ability to lead and inspire. You need to incorporate mechanisms that make it effortless to build cohesiveness and continuity into your day-to-day operations. When you truly believe that your people are your most important assets, you will want to integrate their ideas into your business.

In this chapter, you learned how to introduce and conduct five consultative dialogues as an ongoing means for eliciting creativity from and inspiring participation by your employees. The *performance dialogue* is the feedback mechanism for constant individual and team improvements. *Weekly team dialogues* convey current events that people learn about and discuss together. *Talent review dialogues* provide the flow of human resources allocations for current and future considerations. During *quarterly business scorecard dialogues*, an assessment of the overall business offers the opportunity to test and revise current and future plans. The vital information for this dialogue comes directly from the *best seller dialogues*, which communicate up-to-date data about the current state of the business.

A disciplined, integrated, well-managed, and well-organized company works efficiently and effectively. Talented entrepreneurs who frequently work on their own may may feel constrained with this proposed discipline. However, after a few experiences with consultative dialogue, you will see the valuable contribution it offers your business.

## QUESTIONS AND ACTIONS FOR YOUR BUSINESS PROFITS

- What are the mechanisms or meetings within your business?

  → Review the purpose and usefulness of these.

- What can you do to create more opportunity for consultative dialogue in your business?

# CHAPTER 13

# What to Do Right Now!

*Do what you do so well that they will want to see it again and bring their friends.*

—Walt Disney, The Walt Disney Company

Are you starting to change the way you think about the direction of your business? Is an image emerging in your mind of how you will move it from being merely successful to a model of peak profitability? If so, this chapter will help you get ready to *do something now*. (If you're not quite there yet, go back and review the seven PROFITS principles and resolve to use the three tools—The Business Reality Change Model, People Processes and Consultative Dialogues.)

You have seen how other companies managed to exceed their profit goals by taking the PROFITS principles to heart and applying the tools diligently. You have learned what works and what does not work for other entrepreneurs and you know what questions to ask and answer in order to move your business forward. Of course, you will have many options and possibilities from which to choose and determining the best alternative is your next step in the process for profitable growth.

You should be ready to test the principles and tools now in *your own* business.

And you may ask—as do many of my clients after we've talked about the various next steps they might take—"What can I do right now?" "Where should I start?" "Which tools are the right tools?" In this chapter I offer you the way to do something now!

Remember Melanie of Environmental Inc.? She revised her operations systems by identifying and applying the priorities that would allow her to keep the #1 spot in her industry. You met Jonas CD/DVD, which transformed its business as the market shifted to online and DVD formats (Chapter 4, *Reality*). As a result, both companies enjoyed soaring returns on investment. And staying the course was the right answer for Peekaboo Child (Chapter 7, *Integration*), which accomplished this by carefully managing and optimizing shifting market trends without designing any strategic alterations at all.

What these companies have in common is they began their journey by *obtaining all the vital information* available about their customers, their potential customers, and their customers' customers. From there they *positioned for growth* within a *reality-based* context, developing their thinking, systems, and processes for the greatest *flexibility* while *integrating* their entire business by linking their systems and decisions. Frequently, they *tested and revised* their strategies and plans, adjusting to current market circumstances. Using best practice *people processes*, they hired and retained excellent employees and purposefully created a culture of cooperation and respect within their businesses.

## MAKING STRATEGIC DECISIONS

Your goal now should center on this single action:

> *Invest in transforming changes to the business that are both high priority and provide a high return on investment.*

Building a more profitable business requires that your invested assets produce a high payout. Simply put, if you do not invest enough and if you do not invest strategically, then you cannot keep up with your competitors. You may need new or enhanced products and services ready to go in the pipeline or your systems may need updating for efficiency.

If you fall behind, it is very difficult to catch up. You need to prioritize any change in the way you do business based on the investment you make. Many times the choice is not easy and there are likely conflicting demands for how to use your capital.

We'll use a 2×2 decision matrix to aid you in deciding on your next action steps. Your key strategic business decisions can center on key points you considered as you read this book. Remember that we are striving to boost your business to its maximum profit potential by becoming fully focused on the intersection of what is most profitable for your customer and what is most profitable for your business. Therefore, the decision matrix that I've developed (shown in Figure 13.1) helps you to systematically identify your strategic opportunities and choices, decide whether to take actions, and choose what actions to take.

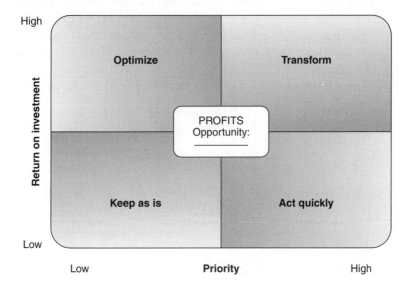

**Figure 13.1** Decision Matrix

**235**

This matrix helps you move beyond your first instinct to focus on the most pressing problem or greatest opportunity. Not all problems require the same investment of time and money. For example, you may have a product line that is losing market share. Do you want to invest more money in this product or do you want to leave it as is or even liquidate the product to use the money elsewhere? When you stop to think about it, the answer depends on what else is happening with your business. You may have another product that is selling well, generating high margins, and projecting a continuous high revenue stream for the next few years. Further investment in the successful product may be a better alternative than adding money to a sinking ship.

How do you know what to do? It's simple: Stay focused on the single idea stated earlier:

> ***Invest in transforming changes to the business that are both high priority and provide a high return on investment.***

If you think about your business options based on a systematic evaluation of priorities and return on investment, the decision process is less risky. As you complete the matrix, notice which areas of your business are both high-priority and providing a high return on investment. Then you can decide on your logical next steps.

Before you can apply the matrix to your own situation, let's define the components and how each one relates to your business.

## Priorities

Because you have limited investment resources, your priorities must lead to creation of customer value. The questions to ask are:

*How will this change benefit the customer?*
*How do I know this?*

The priorities you choose may cause you to consider a strategic change in direction or operational actions that result in changes that make your processes more efficient and produce greater margins and/or pricing adjustments.

## Return on Investment

Your investable assets are financial, people, time, and other resources.

The four quadrants of the matrix represent options for actions you can take *right now*. As mentioned earlier, you must first assess your business. The most comprehensive approach for the assessment is using the Business Reality Change Model (Chapter 10).

Next, determine your problem or opportunity and your frame of reference. Then, summarize the results of your Business Reality Change Model into the relevant quadrants of the matrix, determining the key takeaways from the assessment about the *return on investment (high or low)* and *priority (high or low)* for each option for taking action in solving your problem or opportunity.

Each component you place within the decision matrix should suggest a possible action. These definitions will help you evaluate your options:

### Keep As Is

If your business is running well and no pressing problems are on the horizon, you may be satisfied to remain at your current level of profitability and not make changes to grow your business.

If you have assigned many possibilities to this quadrant, however, you may need to question whether you have become complacent. You may want to ask yourself: *Are you and your employees missing opportunities to create greater customer value?* The key learning is to be certain you have chosen, rather than drifted into, the *Keep As Is* mode of operating.

### Optimize

If your profitability is the result of efficient and effective operations, then return on investment is high and there is low priority to change at this time. The message of this quadrant is to keep your eye on the ball and manage your current situation well.

Optimize your actions by ensuring continuous efficiency and improvement. You must always guard against complacency, so keep abreast of market trends and changes. Remember, your assessment is limited by your frame of reference.

### Act Quickly

Within this quadrant, your business faces an immediate threat from within or from outside market forces. If you miss the opportunity to act quickly, you may never recoup revenue or market share lost to the threat. Threats can be new entrants or competitors that emerge in the market with a superior solution or unanticipated expenses that may reduce the funds available to address the threat. A key employee may leave; sales may fall, you may misread the market, your customers' market may change unexpectedly, or there may be a change in government regulations you must address.

Though the return on investment for changes required to meet any of these threats may be low, the survival of your business may require that you do them anyway—and right away. If you don't, the loss may be greater.

### Transform

A solution in this quadrant requires a dramatic strategic shift. Return on investment is high when the solution is effective. Action is a high priority here, because to remain a key player in the marketplace, you must change. It is wise to consider the risks (which you probably already did when you worked the Business Reality Change Model), since this is a dramatic strategic shift. If you find that the risks are too high, you might reconsider transformation as an option at this time. You may not have the core capabilities available right now. The transformation may be too disruptive for your employees. You may not have sufficient funding commitments. However, knowing that a dramatic shift is important for your company's future, this matrix becomes your road map to taking the actions required to get prepared and position your company for the transformation as quickly as you can.

*Keep in mind that circumstances can change quickly.* Focusing on one quadrant can affect another and your marketplace can shift in a matter of weeks or months.

To utilize the decision matrix as a primary business tool, I suggest you work through the exercise every three months. Pay attention to how your criteria for business priorities and return on investment change over time. Taking action early keeps you on track and ahead of your competitors.

An even more comprehensive way to assess your situation is to think in terms of the PROFITS principles and fill out a matrix for each letter (P, R, O, F, I, T, S) for the most comprehensive analysis.

Shoppers Square's decision matrix analysis for *Flexibility* (Chapter 6) is shown in Figure 13.2.

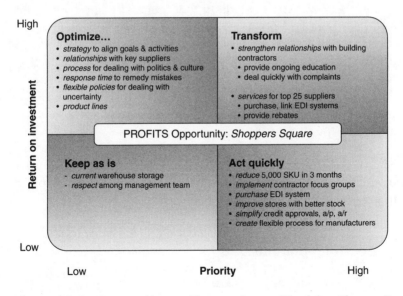

**Figure 13.2** Decision Matrix—Shoppers Square (*Flexibility*, Chapter 6)

The information in each quadrant provides a way to visualize both your priorities and the return on investment. In the Shoppers Square case, reducing 5,000 SKUs is in the *Act Quickly* quadrant. Since reducing 5,000 SKUs is supposed to be an improvement for Shoppers Square, you might ask why it is in the *Act Quickly* Quadrant, which represents low return on investment.

The fact is that many times when we introduce change, profits may stagnate or even decline for a time. Once the change is executed and people are up to speed, profits rise quickly and make up for the initial plateau or decrease. This was indeed the case with Shoppers Square. The reduction of 5,000 SKUs had to happen very quickly since evidence indicated that too many SKUs were confusing existing customers and there was no time to wait to fix this. At that point, change was urgent even if execution was not ideal. When companies *Act Quickly* they need to pay attention and formulate improvements as the change takes place and even after the initial change occurs.

Although you may run into some of the same issues that require continuous improvement after a change takes place within the *Transform* Quadrant, you generally have more time to think about and position your decision to make changes.

After completing your decision matrix analysis, you should be able to determine your *profitable* next step. Some actions will be evident from the analysis, whereas others may require that you conduct research into various business models. The outcome depends most on how candidly and thoroughly you approach the exercise.

The following are some possible solutions for transforming all or parts of your business once you have your decision matrix organized. While these are some of the more obvious solutions to get you started, you may come up with several more on your own.

**Possible Solutions:**

- Do nothing and keep as is.
- Hire a consulting company to do the work.

- Hire more staff.
- Add the missing capability (buy or develop it).
- Obtain financing.
- Merge with another company.
- Acquire another company.
- Form strategic alliances with other companies.
- Outsource the function needed.
- Sell the company.

As you mull over possible next steps about *what to do right now* to move your company to a higher level of profitability, I would like to share the current journey of Q Products, Inc.

## Q PRODUCTS, INC.

There are many reasons why Jonathan Soares' story is important, but none more compelling than the fact that it expresses how a dream nurtured within one soul, backed with solid plans to make it happen with persistence over the long haul *will* make that dream come true. Q Products, Inc. is the equivalent of an entrepreneur's *Field of Dreams*.

In 2005, with a $10,000 investment and his family's barbecue sauce recipes, Jonathan Soares launched Q Products' premium BBQ sauces in the $351 million condiment industry. He focused his energy and time on sales, marketing, and coordinating strategic outsourced relationships with a local Connecticut manufacturing production facility and a national logistics company.

Though I did not know Jonathan when he first began his journey, we both recognized when we got to know one another that he indeed exemplified all of the PROFITS principles. He dealt with the *reality* of a competitive industry, *positioning Q Products for growth* in the premium condiment category for healthy, environmentally conscious gourmet consumers.

With an eye toward creating a long-term profitable business and the ambition to make it happen, Jonathan did his research. He *obtained vital information* by speaking to successful businesspeople and extrapolating their secrets of success. Then, he formed a board of directors to leverage the advice of others and a holding company that *positioned him for continuing growth* within his current business model. The holding company, designed for maximum *flexibility* in the business model, positions Q Products, Inc. to add new products when the time is right. With a fail-safe plan built in for company *integration* with *testing and revising* mechanisms, the Q Products, Inc. holding company can adapt and act as the market shifts. After three years of profitable growth and astute decision making (allowing the company to be driven by the market and customers, rather than products), Q Products readied for the next level of growth.

Jonathan's strategic insights led him to seek funding once he had a strong record of accomplishment. This meant moving beyond the image of small business entrepreneur and positioning himself as a formidable competitor among mainstream brands.

When Jonathan reviewed the PROFITS principles and completed a Business Reality Change Model analysis, he chose to focus on his current opportunity: *how to generate volume and create sustainable profits within two months in the Southeastern states*. He chose the Southeast as his pilot for *testing and revising* his plans because of several new opportunities existing there, even though he understood that various regions of the country would pose different challenges.

Relying on external, internal, and subsequent SWOT analyses, Jonathan went beyond top-level goals by creating objectives and measures. He then directed his efforts to growing his customer base by strengthening consumer relationships, increasing store penetration, and aggressively pricing his products throughout the manufacturing, distribution, and retail channels. With the success of the Southeast pilot, Jonathan was able to expand his plans nationwide.

As he continues to *test and revise* his plans for each region of the United States, Jonathan fine-tunes the strategy and plans for Q Products. Now with a national presence in 4,500 stores,

Q Products projects revenues of $30 million in 2011. Q's new business model achieves 60 percent in gross margin compared with the previous 40 percent. A strategic manufacturing partnership increased production capacity and a logistics partner with end-to-end supply chain capability provides *growth positioning*, *flexibility*, and *integration*. With the hiring of two more excellent executives for his management team, Jonathan coordinates his company to operate with even greater efficiency and effectiveness—*steering the company* with values, interpersonal savvy, and innovation to achieve $30 million in potential revenues.

What is the lesson you can learn from Q Products? In my experience, the burning challenge for entrepreneurs like you is to balance the immediate challenges with long-term goals. Sometimes all it takes is recognizing the effects that the choices you make now will have on business in the future—and discover how to structure and sequence those choices.

Successful Fortune 100 companies perform this balancing act continuously by breaking down key operational and strategic goals into actionable chunks and applying business logic in deciding what to do and when to do it. Using PROFITS principles and the tools is how *you* will get there, too.

This book is my tribute to you—entrepreneurs everywhere with passionate dreams and the energy to make them happen!

# Bibliography

## CHAPTER 1: ACHIEVING A PROFITABLE BUSINESS

Collins, J. *Good to Great: Why Some Companies Make the Leap . . . and Others Don't*. New York: Collins Business, 2001.

Friedman, T. L. *The World Is Flat*. Updated & expanded ed. New York: Farrar, Straus & Giroux, 2006.

Gladwell, M. *The Tipping Point: How Little Things Can Make a Big Difference*. New York: Little, Brown, 2000.

Pink, D. *Free Agent Nation: How America's New Independent Workers Are Transforming the Way We Live*. New York: Warner Books, 2001.

Raynor, M. E. *The Strategy Paradox: Why Committing to Success Leads to Failure (and What to Do about It)*. New York: Doubleday Business, 2007.

## CHAPTER 2: PROFITS

Collins, J. *Good to Great: Why Some Companies Make the Leap . . . and Others Don't*. New York: Collins Business, 2001.

## CHAPTER 3: POSITION ONLY FOR GROWTH

Christensen, C. M., and M. E. Raynor. *The Innovator's Solution: Creating and Sustaining Successful Growth*. Boston: Harvard Business School Press, 2003.

Kim, W. C., and R. Mauborgne. *Blue Ocean Strategy: How to Create Uncontested Market Space and Make Competition Irrelevant*. Boston: Harvard Business School Press, 2005.

Porter, M. E. *Competitive Advantage: Creating and Sustaining Superior Performance*. New York: Free Press, 1998.

Porter, M. E. *Competitive Strategy: Techniques for Analyzing Industries and Competitors*. New York: Free Press, 1998.

Porter, M. E. *On Competition*. Boston: Harvard Business School Press, 2008.

Ross, S. A., R. W. Westerfield, and B. D. Jordan. *Fundamentals of Corporate Finance*. 8th ed. New York: Irwin/McGraw-Hill, 2008.

Slywotzky, A. J., D. J. Morrison, and B. Andelman. *The Profit Zone: How Strategic Business Design Will Lead You to Tomorrow's Profit*. New York: Three Rivers Press, 2002.

Stiglitz, J. E. *Economics*. New York: W. W. Norton, 2006.

Zook, C. *Unstoppable: Finding Hidden Assets to Renew the Core and Fuel Profitable Growth*. Boston: Harvard Business School Press, 2007.

Zook, C., and J. Allen. *Profit from the Core: Growth Strategy in an Era of Turbulence*. Boston: Harvard Business School Press, 2001.

## CHAPTER 4: REALITY

Bossidy, L., R. Charan, and C. Burck. *Execution: The Discipline of Getting Things Done*. New York: Crown Business, 2002.

Collins, J., and J. I. Porras. *Built to Last: Successful Habits of Visionary Companies*. New York: Collins Business, 2004.

Connellan, T. *Inside the Magic Kingdom: Seven Keys to Disney's Success*. Austin, TX: Bard Press, 1997.

Janis, I. L. *Groupthink: Psychological Studies of Policy Decisions and Fiascoes*. Boston: Houghton Mifflin, 1982.

Ross, S. A., R. W. Westerfield, and B. D. Jordan. *Fundamentals of Corporate Finance*. 8th ed. New York: Irwin/McGraw-Hill, 2008.

# BIBLIOGRAPHY

## CHAPTER 5: OBTAIN VITAL INFORMATION

Crenshaw, D. *The Myth of Multitasking: How "Doing It All" Gets Nothing Done*. San Francisco: Jossey-Bass, 2008.

Kelley, R. E. *How to Be a Star at Work: 9 Breakthrough Strategies You Need to Succeed*. New York: Three Rivers Press, 1999.

Mackay, H. *Dig Your Well Before You're Thirsty: The Only Networking Book You'll Ever Need*. New York: Doubleday Business, 1999.

Pattison, K. "Work Interrupted: The Cost of Task Switching." *Fast Company*, July 28, 2008.

Rubinstein, J. S., D. E. Meyer, and J. E. Evans. "Executive Control of Cognitive Processes in Task Switching." *Journal of Experimental Psychology—Human Perception and Performance* 27(4).

Weber, L. *Marketing to the Social Web: How Digital Customer Communities Build Your Business*. Hoboken, NJ: John Wiley & Sons, 2007.

## CHAPTER 6: FLEXIBILITY

Argyris, C. *Overcoming Organizational Defenses: Facilitating Organizational Learning*. Upper Saddle River, NJ: Prentice-Hall, 1990.

Argyris, C. *Reasons and Rationalizations: The Limits to Organizational Knowledge*. New York: Oxford University Press, 2006.

De Bono, E. *Six Thinking Hats: An Essential Approach to Business Management*. New York: Back Bay Books, 1999.

De Bono, E. *Tactics*. New York: HarperCollins, 1996; Profile Business, 2007.

Sheahan, P. *Flip: How to Turn Everything You Know on Its Head—and Succeed Beyond Your Wildest Imaginings*. New York: William Morrow, 2008.

## CHAPTER 7: INTEGRATION

Hackman, R. *Leading Teams: Setting the Stage for Great Performances*. Boston: Harvard Business School Press, 2002.

Hammer, M. *The Agenda: What Every Business Must Do to Dominate the Decade*. New York: Three Rivers Press, 2003.

Kaplan, R. S., and D. P. Norton. *The Balanced Scorecard: Translating Strategy into Action*. Boston: Harvard Business School Press, 1996.

Kelly, J. N., and F. J. Gouillart. *Transforming the Organization*. New York: McGraw-Hill, 1995.

Mohammed, R. *The Art of Pricing: How to Find the Hidden Profits to Grow Your Business*. New York: Crown Business, 2005.

Slywotzky, A. J., D. J. Morrison, and B. Andelman. *The Profit Zone: How Strategic Business Design Will Lead You to Tomorrow's Profit*. New York: Three Rivers Press, 2002.

## CHAPTER 8: TEST AND REVISE

Meister, J. *Building a Learning Organization*. Nebraska: iUniverse, 2001.

Mohammed, R. *The Art of Pricing: How to Find the Hidden Profits to Grow Your Business*. New York: Crown Business, 2005.

Charan, R., *Boards That Deliver*. San Francisco: Jossey-Bass. 2005.

## CHAPTER 9: STEERING THE COMPANY

Charan, R., S. Drotter, and J. Noel. *The Leadership Pipeline: How to Build the Leadership Powered Company*. San Francisco: Jossey-Bass, 2000.

Kelley, R. E., *How to Be a Star at Work: 9 Breakthrough Strategies You Need to Succeed*. New York: Three Rivers Press, 1999.

Schein, E. H. *Organizational Culture and Leadership* (Business & Management Series). San Francisco: Jossey-Bass, 2004.

Senge, P. M. *The Fifth Discipline: The Art & Practice of the Learning Organization*. New York: Doubleday Business, 2006.

Tichy, N. M., and W. G. Bennis. *Judgment: How Winning Leaders Make Great Calls*. New York: Portfolio/Penguin, 2007.

## CHAPTER 11: PEOPLE PROCESSES

Dychtwald, K., T. E. Erickson, and R. Morison. *Workforce Crisis: How to Beat the Coming Shortage of Skills and Talent*. Boston: Harvard Business Press, 2006.

Goleman, D., R. E. Boyatzis, and A. McKee. *Primal Leadership: Learning to Lead with Emotional Intelligence.* Boston: Harvard Business Press 2004.

## CHAPTER 12: CONSULTATIVE DIALOGUES

Argyris, C. *Overcoming Organizational Defenses: Facilitating Organizational Learning.* Upper Saddle River, NJ: Prentice-Hall, 1990.

Argyris, C. *Reasons and Rationalizations: The Limits to Organizational Knowledge.* New York: Oxford University Press, 2006.

Isaksen, S. G., & G. Ekvall, with H. Akkermans, G. Wilson, and J. Gaulin. *Assessing the Context for Change: A Technical Manual for the Situational Outlook Questionnaire.* Orchard Park, NY: Creative Problem Solving Group, 2007.

# Index

Accountability:
  autonomy, 107, 128–132, 166
  cross-functional, 87–91, 118–120
  philosophy of, 119
  ownership, 22, 32, 63, 86, 92, 198, 209, 220
  rewards, 131–132
  training, 133–135
Accounting Inc., 23–25, 29
Airplane metaphor, 153
Alliances:
  external, 89–91, 95
  internal, 89–90
Assumptions:
  questioning, 71–73

Babies R Us, 145
Baldwin Mediaworks, 93–94, 149
Brainstorming, 222–225
Business:
  Acumen, 13–19
  amenities, 122–123, 142
  complexity, 13, 45, 57–59, 241
  consortiums, 103–104, 111–112
  core capabilities, 67–75, 81–82, 203–216, 226, 234
  excellence, 142–143
  expansion, 4, 6, 14, 23, 40, 118, 146
  flexibility, 93–99

integration, 117–135, 241
limitations, 111–113, 184–189
model, 36–37, 166–169, 189–190, 232
report card, 226–227
strategy, 47, 137, 141, 231
Business Reality Change model, 15–16, 177–193, 202–224
B to Z glass, 87–88

Change, 98–100, 164–170
  champion, 96, 100, 115
  market, 46, 75, 175
  planned change, 100
  resistance, 25, 27, 153, 165–167, 170
  strategic, 234–236
Children's clothing, 146
Citibank, 46–47, 54, 145
Clemens Boatworks, 53, 140–141
Collaboration, 109, 146–147
Collins, Jim, 11
Communication:
  focus, 92–94
  priorities, 104
  transparency, 108–112
Company culture:
  assessments, 180–181, 195–197, 227, 233–234
  beliefs, 130–131, 152–154

Company culture (*Continued*)
 discipline, 97–98, 118–120, 227
 dysfunction, 160–166
 flexibility, 96–100
 health, 156, 166–167, 170
 history, 42, 129–132
 learning, 96–100, 129–131
 loyalty, 106, 163, 167, 188–189
 mission, 14, 25, 27, 82, 87, 93–94,
  100, 118–119, 132
 objection to corporate, 8–9
 reviews, 137–138
 trust, 119, 164
 values, 152–154, 206, 239
Company vulnerabilities, 182–184,
  188, 199–200
Competency development, 196–198,
  204–205, 207–218
Competitive,
 challenges, 19–23, 110–111,
  238–239
 reality, 45–51, 97–107, 186–187,
  234–235
 shifts, 35, 50–54
Constituencies:
 key, 132–136
Consultative dialogue, 168–170,
  216–229, 242
Container company, 49, 107, 183
Contingency planning, 125, 147–150
CopperPlumbing, 35–37,
  59–60
Costco, 52, 102
Cross–selling, 47–48
Commitment, 84–86
Corporate University Xchange, 196
Customers:
 constraints, 48–49, 54
 feedback, 101–102, 123–124
 intelligence, 84–88
 perspective, 140–142
 resistance, 85–86
 service, 48–50, 82, 104–105, 109,
  120

 their customers, 86–88, 123,
 value chain, 123

Dancing with the Stars,
  114–115
Data anomalies, 82–83
Decisions, 6, 12, 19, 28, 43–47,
  119–122
 decision matrix, 230–236
Deliveries, 63, 79, 99, 108, 125, 134,
  139
Disasters:
 chaos, 66, 98, 110, 178, 195
 coping with, 20, 55, 62–65, 70, 98,
  160
Distractions, 120, 125–126, 135–138,
  144
Diversity workshops, 167

Early adopters, 99–100
Employee,
 derailment, 200, 208–210, 215
 incentive, 149
 loyalty, 159
 mobilizing, 62–65, 149, 161, 196,
  208–210
 participation, 117
 performance, 195, 203
 retention, 129, 134
 suggestions, 106–108
 turnover, 49
Energizer Fitness, 26–27
Environmental Inc., 18–20, 27–28,
  49, 138–142, 230

Facilitator, 222–224
FDIC, 167
Financial:
 cost centers, 58, 127–128
 expenditures, 48–49, 54
 growth, 4, 13–14, 22–29, 34–41,
  237–238
 inventory turnover, 59–63, 120,
  138, 145, 186–187

margins, operating, 142–143
measures, 42–44, 53–57, 126,
    128–129, 183, 187
performance, 34, 41–45, 48–50, 53
revenue, 35–38, 127–129, 226–227
risk, 36–37, 70–71
velocity, 44–45, 227
scorecards, 128, 218, 226–227
Flexibility:
change, 96–102
effectiveness, 98
speed, 99
Friedman, Thomas, 12

Gerard's team, 156
Gerstner, Louis, 11
Gladwell, Malcolm, 11–12
Goals, 7, 9–10
    agreement, 66–70, 149–50
    clarity, 148–149, 157–160
    correlation of, 166–131
Goleman, Dan, 196
Gore Associates, 129–131, 153, 157
Governance, 141, 148–50

Hallmark Entertainment, 102
Henry Ford, 159
High potential/performer, 193–198,
    211–216
Home goods, 63–64, 109,
    124–126,144,154, 162
    Linens–n–Things, 51
    Bed Bath & Beyond, 51
Hurricane Katrina, 63–67

Imaging equipment, 36–37
Information centers:
    deciphering, 130–131
    exchange, 218
    linking systems, 133–134
    information networks,
    135
Innovation, 36–39, 153, 165–170,
    239

Insurance:
    AIG, 58–59
    Amsen Insurers, 20
    Doug, 122–123
Internal:
    consistency, 126–127, 135
    systems, 34, 48–50, 54, 73
Investors, 37, 56, 97, 111–112, 130,
    140

Jonas, CD/DVD, 56, 97

Kravitts, Jim, 8, 177–178
Kreitman, David, 50, 103–104,
    111–113

La Valore Cosmetics, 90–91
Leadership, 16, 129, 154, 192–196,
    206
    competencies, 204–207
    employee development, 104–108,
    147–150, 159–167, 207–218
Logistics, 10, 49, 108, 183, 226
Lucky Paints, 160–161

Market research, 26, 183
Measuring:
    behavior, 127–129,163–170, 228
    results, 104–105, 135, 202–205
Meditation exercise, 153–156
Mercy Hospital, 102
Multitasking, 83–84, 94

Nantucket Frocks, 53–54
Networking, 78–79, 89–95, 109,
    209

Obary Steel, 74–75
Organizational dysfunction, 161–162
Outsourcing, 24, 29, 36, 49, 73–75,
    193
    Inefficiencies, 73–75

PackPlus, 107–108, 145